THE LIVES THEY
LEFT BEHIND

THE LIVES THEY LEFT BEHIND

SUITCASES FROM A STATE HOSPITAL ATTIC

Darby Penney and Peter Stastny

With Photographs by Lisa Rinzler

BELLEVUE LITERARY PRESS
NEW YORK

AUTHORS' NOTE

We would have preferred to honor the memories of the suitcase owners by using their full names; unfortunately, confidentiality laws made that impossible. Instead, we have used their real first names and reluctantly chosen pseudonymous last names that reflect their ethnicities and national origins.

First published in the United States in 2008 by
Bellevue Literary Press
New York

FOR INFORMATION ADDRESS:
Bellevue Literary Press
NYU School of Medicine
550 First Avenue
OBV 640
New York, NY 10016

PHOTO CREDITS: Photographs on pages 21-22, 33 (top)35-36, 40, 47, 55, 57, 73, 80, 99, 103-104, 106-108, 111, 114, 126, 142, 175, 177, 180, courtesy of the New York State Archives; 47-48, 50, 88, 90, 93-94, 115, 118, 128, 130, 149, 161-165, 170-171, courtesy of the New York State Museum; Photograph on p. 133 by Peter Stastny. All other photographs are by Lisa Rinzler.

This book was published with the generous support of Bellevue Literary Press's founding donor the Arnold Simon Family Trust, the Bernard & Irene Schwartz Foundation, the Lucius N. Littauer Foundation and the van Ameringen Foundation.

Cataloging-in-Publication Data is available from the Library of Congress

Book design and type formatting by Bernard Schleifer
Manufactured in the United States of America
ISBN 1-934137-07-9
FIRST EDITION
1 3 5 7 9 8 6 4 2

This book is dedicated to the memories of the Willard suitcase owners, and to all others who have lived and died in mental institutions.

CONTENTS

FOREWORD

The literature on the history of our country's treatment of people it considers mad basically consists of two types of books. There are histories that tell of the various medical therapies and types of institutional care that have been employed to treat those with mental and emotional problems over the past two hundred years, and then there are a handful of memoirs by current and former patients, nearly all of which raise troubling questions about the humanity of those "treatments." The perspective that has always gone missing is an outsider's look, in the manner of a journalist or historian, at the lives of individual patients. What are their life stories? How did they end up in an asylum or mental hospital? How did the "treatment" change their lives?

Now we have such a book in *The Lives They Left Behind*. Through years of diligent research, Peter Stastny and Darby Penney have uncovered and documented the personal stories of people who spent decades at Willard State Hospital. Theirs is a stunning achievement, for they have written a book that bears witness—and in the most powerful manner possible—to a tragic time.

The history of our country's treatment of people with mental and emotional distress is a troubled one. At the moment of our country's founding, Benjamin Rush and other prominent colonial physicians utilized the modern "treatments" they'd learned about from their studies in England—therapies that were often extremely aggressive. The prevailing thought was that those deemed mad, by virtue of the fact that they had lost their "reason," had descended to the level of a beast, and so English "mad doctors" had long advised that the "insane" needed to be "tamed" and "weakened." Rush bled his patients profusely, and kept them tightly bound in a "tranquilizer chair" for long hours, this latter treatment hailed for making even the most irascible patient "gentle and submissive."

Around 1800, Quakers in York, England, upset with such harsh therapeutics, pioneered an alternative form of care known as moral therapy. The

Quakers reasoned that while they didn't know what caused madness, those who were suffering were still "brethren" and should be treated as such. They built a small retreat in the country, where they sought to treat their patients with kindness and provide them with shelter, good food, and companionship. Quakers in Boston, Philadelphia, and other cities soon built similar retreats, and modern historians have concluded that this form of gentle care worked well: more than 50 percent of the "newly insane" would be discharged within a year, and in the best long-term study of moral therapy that was ever done, researchers reported that 58 percent of those so discharged never returned to a hospital again.

The success of moral therapy ironically led to its downfall. Dorothea Dix, a nineteenth-century reformer from Massachusetts, lobbied state legislatures to build state asylums to provide this care to all who needed it, only once they did, cities and towns began dumping all sorts of people into these facilities. Elderly people, those with syphilis who had end-stage dementia, and those with incurable neurological disorders joined the "newly insane" in these mental hospitals, which grew ever larger and more crowded. Discharge rates naturally fell as this happened, and by the end of the century "moral therapy" had come to be seen as a failed therapy, asylum doctors having forgotten how, only fifty years earlier, it was common for the "newly insane" to recover and to never be rehospitalized.

This brings us to the period that is the subject of this book: 1900 to 1950. It is, in some ways, the darkest period in American history in terms of our treatment of people diagnosed with mental illness.

As the twentieth century dawned, America was falling under the sway of eugenic conceptions of "mental illness." Eugenicists argued that if a society wanted to prosper, it needed to encourage those with good "germ plasm"—those the eugenicists deemed the "fittest"—to breed, and to discourage those with bad "germ plasm" from having offspring. Those deemed mentally ill were naturally seen as among the most "unfit," and so eugenicists argued that they should be segregated in mental hospitals. The hospital was no longer seen as a refuge for troubled people, but rather as a place for keeping them away from society during their breeding years so they would not pass along their "bad germ plasm." Eugenicists also touted the notion that insanity was a single gene disorder, and thus it was hopeless to think an "insane" person could ever recover.

As a result of these eugenic beliefs, mental hospital discharge rates plummeted. Whereas more than half of the newly diagnosed treated in the early moral therapy asylums would be discharged within a year, patients in the first half of the twentieth century spent decades in state mental hospitals. For instance, a 1931 study of 5,164 first-episode patients admitted to New York hospitals from 1909 to 1911 found that over the next seventeen years, only 42 percent were ever discharged. The remaining 58 percent either died in the hospital or were still confined at the end of that period. As a result, the number of people in state hospitals rose from 126,000 in 1900 to 419,000 in 1940. A person admitted to a state hospital during this period had every reason to fear he would never get out.

The Lives They Left Behind tells the life stories of ten of those people. The tragedy of that era is illuminated in this book in a way no statistics ever could. The photos are equally haunting, and together they document a time when those who struggled with their minds, and often for the most common of reasons—loss of a loved one, loss of a job, or the difficulties that came with being an immigrant in a strange land—were locked away in mental hospitals and then forgotten.

It is tempting to look back at that era and see only the shameful relics of a distant past. Today, we tell ourselves, we are much more "humane" in our treatment of those with mental health problems, and our therapies are better, too. Yet any close examination of our care today should give us pause. The World Health Organization has twice found that schizophrenia outcomes are much, much better in poor countries like India, Nigeria, and Colombia than in the United States and other rich countries. Moreover, the number of psychiatrically disabled people in the United States has increased from 600,000 in 1955 to nearly six million today, a statistic that shows we still do not have a form of care that truly helps people recover, and even suggests that we are doing something today that may actively prevent recovery.

Perhaps Darby Penney and Peter Stastny will turn their attention to that conundrum next. This book illuminates the tragedy of our treatment of those with mental and emotional problems during the first half of the twentieth century in a novel and unforgettable way.

—ROBERT WHITAKER
Author of *Mad in America*

Willard State Hospital, aerial view, ca. 1980s

PROLOGUE:
LIFE IN THE ATTIC

T he Sheltered Workshop Building stands alone on a hill overlooking Seneca Lake next to the empty lot that once held Chapin Hall, the massive central building of Willard State Hospital in New York. When that towering, meandering structure was torn down in 1988, the institution lost its architectural heart, leaving a scattered bunch of buildings that housed nearly a thousand mental patients until the state finally decided to abandon the entire facility in 1995. That spring, all remaining patients were distributed to other institutions. Curators and state workers roamed the grounds, trying to safeguard anything that might be worth keeping before the buildings were condemned. They scurried from building to building, determined to beat the looming deadline of the demolition crews.

Beverly Courtwright and Lisa Hoffman, two local women who worked at Willard, knew the place intimately. They guided Craig Williams, a curator from the New York State Museum, to the spots that offered the most promise for finding important artifacts. Beverly remembered that there was something stashed under the roof of the Sheltered Workshop Building. She led the group up the steep staircase to the attic and then to a door in a partition under pigeon-infested rafters. Once the door was pried open, they were struck by an awesome sight: a beam of sunlight streaming down a central corridor that separated rows of wooden racks tightly filled with suitcases of all shapes and sizes—men's on the left side, women's on the right, alphabetized, labeled, and covered by layers of bird droppings, apparently untouched for a great many years.

Crates, trunks, hundreds of standard suitcases, doctor's bags, and many-shaped containers were all neatly arrayed under the watchful eyes of the pigeons who had come to join the lost souls and their worldly possessions. For Beverly and some others who saw it, this upper room exuded an unearthly air, a hovering presence of hundreds of souls or spirits attached

to the many people who had handled and worn the items in those bags before they were packed, who had read the books, written in the diaries, and looked into the mirrors they contained.

Craig Williams, realizing that he had stumbled across a dream of a treasure, called for additional trucks to salvage the luggage. "Just keep ten, and throw the rest away," he was told. Fortunately, Craig ignored this order, and within hours, all 427 suitcases were wrapped in plastic and driven to the museum's warehouse. He knew this was a unique historical find, but one that could not be dealt with immediately. Interns and volunteers cataloged the items in some of the suitcases over the next three years, but the majority of them remained unopened.

In 1998, a group of archivists and curators, including Craig Williams, met with officials of the New York State Office of Mental Health to brief them on a ten-year plan to document the history of mental health in the state. Almost as an aside, Craig mentioned the patient suitcases in the museum's warehouse from the Willard attic that were saved from destruction when the facility closed in 1995.

This is where we—the authors—come in. One person at the meeting, Darby Penney, recognized the potential of this historic find to shed light on the lives of forgotten mental patients. She was Director of Recipient Affairs, a position created in the early 1990s to facilitate input from current and former patients about policies and programs. Darby invited her colleague Peter

Stastny, a psychiatrist and documentary filmmaker, to join the project. Peter brought in photographer Lisa Rinzler to guide the team's visual approach. This collaboration resulted in a major exhibit at the New York State Museum in 2004, attended by over 600,000 visitors; a website (*www.SuitcaseExhibit .org*); a traveling exhibit; and, ultimately, this book.

On our first ride up to Willard, catching a view of two lakes, one before us, the other in our rearview mirror, we could never imagine the worlds that would open up behind the fences, walls, and leather latches.

By then half of the facility had been converted to a boot camp for drug-addicted state prisoners. As we drove onto the grounds, we heard their marching chants in the background. Some buildings were nailed shut. Others were still open, housing workers, alcoholics, a day-care center, but no psychiatric patients. Oddly enough, we noticed a group of obvious patients with their medication shuffle and their poor clothing at a campground by the lake. Some of them were former Willard patients who had come here for an outing from Elmira Psychiatric Center, thirty miles to the south, where many Willard patients had been moved when the facility closed.

We pulled up to the Sheltered Workshop Building and waited for the woman with the keys. Once again, it was Beverly who took us up to her aerie. The old freight elevator had been out of service for years. The huge workshop tables, once surrounded by patients packing pens or gluing paper

bags, stood empty in the barren halls. Old calendars, fire extinguishers last inspected a decade ago, hung on the walls. The staircase was steep, but we trudged up with our camera equipment. Breathless and struggling with dust, we arrived at the top. A few suitcases and clothes were strewn next to a window on the east side of the attic—a strange mixture of beauty and neglect.

Bending under the low rafters, we reached the door in the partition wall and opened it. It was late afternoon. Snow had fallen through an open latch. Rows of empty racks took up the entire space, still labeled "Men" and "Women," and lettered *A* through *Z* on each side. An old lab coat hung from a nail, a strangely human shell overseeing it all. Haste had left behind several gutted suitcases, broken interiors of steamer trunks with Chinese motifs, their contents spilling onto the wood floor, mingling with dust and snow, house keys, photographs, earrings, and belts.

We spent much time exploring and documenting the place where the suitcase owners had spent their lives; clambered into basements, scaled several other pigeon-infested attics, and toured dozens of abandoned wards. We tried to hit some pins in the hospital's bowling alley, timidly traipsed through its morgue, and unearthed discarded old grave markers in the

gully behind the burial grounds. But nothing else had anywhere near the potency of that attic. When we brought a bunch of empty suitcases back up to re-create the time when they were all stacked there, we realized that the space had been irrevocably violated once that door was opened. The spirits of the suitcase owners had been awakened without their consent, and we felt that we owed them our utmost effort to do them justice.

The vast museum warehouse in Rotterdam, New York, became our operating theater where we encountered the suitcases wrapped in dusty sheets of white plastic, multiply tagged, and piled high among the antique cars, building facades, agricultural relics, and thousands of other artifacts from New York State's history. Working with a list of names and hospital identification numbers, we went through

Discarded grave markers, Willard Cemetery

First view of Lawrence Marek's suitcase

several hundred containers, separating the empty ones from those that held merely a sewing kit or a pocket knife. Our mission was to choose a relatively small number of suitcase owners for closer study, and we did not want to miss those who left fewer items behind. There were some obvious choices: the eighteen pieces of luggage that belonged to one woman and included much of her furnishings; several oversize steamer trunks, footlockers, wardrobes, upright ladies' Saratoga trunks (so named because they could hold enough clothes for an entire summer season in the resort town of Saratoga Springs, New York), and a good dozen doctors' bags. These drew our attention not just because of their sizes and unusual shapes, but also for their elaborate markings, monograms, and signs of extensive travel. When opened, dense collections of personal items spilled from many of these suitcases, sometimes still in the same position as they were packed, others obviously disturbed during the intervening years.

By the time we had gone through all 427 cataloged containers, we chose 25 individuals for further study, either because their belongings called out to us in a loud and clear manner, or because the relatively few items remaining in their trunks hinted at unique personal traits and backgrounds. This was the case for one embossed leather suitcase containing just a pair of dress shoes, galoshes, shaving utensils, and a belt, which, had we passed over it, would have deprived us of the opportunity to discover one of the most compelling stories of the lot.

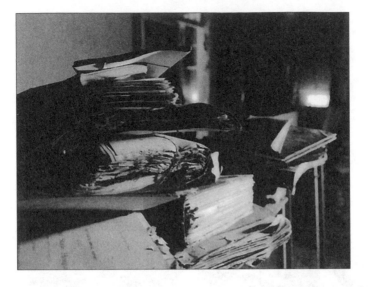

Once we knew who we wanted to focus on, we needed access to their medical records. As part of a research project, we got permission to view the records, which were kept in an abandoned hospital building contaminated by asbestos and lead paint, requiring us to don protective booties, masks, and gowns. Most of the charts were in several volumes, spanning years of institutionalization. Affixed to the front page were passport-size photos of the inmates, alternatingly cheerful and grim, sometimes followed by a photo taken in old age. For the first time, we could look into the people's eyes. Those who smiled at us, like Marie Lehner, seemed oddly inviting, while others churned our hearts: ravaged, toothless, their glances broken. We were only allowed a few hours with those records spanning hundreds of hospital years. We copied pages, caught a few words here and there—"dementia praecox" indelibly etched on the face sheet of a person's life. Correspondence was attached in the back; there were chart entries in dozens of different scripts, colors, and levels of erudition; medication logs, a sea of initials entered to signify that a dose was given, or refused; X-ray reports, the tracings of a beating heart; and postmortem results.

Once we had worked with these files, the hints from the records and the bags began to coalesce into a plan for discovering the suitcase owners' pasts. Hardly anyone had living relatives, and many of their old addresses had been razed by urban renewal. But sometimes we found those long-lost places in a similar state as when their tenants left them behind, like the home of the Sicilian laborer Michael Bastone on a street corner south of the Ithaca rail yards, surrounded by industrial castoffs. We were approached by a man in a pickup truck who turned out to be a son of the neighbor who had called the police on Mr. Bastone more than sixty years ago. Or the twin

Michael Bastone's former residence, Ithaca, New York

brownstones across the street from St. Joseph's Hospital in Syracuse, New York, where Dmytre and Sofia Zarchuk lived and where Sofia died. As we photographed the building, a man emerged from the neighboring house —he was the Zarchuks' Italian landlady's son. His eighty-eight-year-old mother still lived there and remembered her tenant from 1952 as "the beautiful young nurse" from next door. Sometimes all we found was a grave, like that of the photographer Herman Graham in Mount Olivet Cemetery, in Maspeth, Queens, New York, or Ethel Smalls's in Trumansburg, New York.

We had spent our careers speaking up for living people who got caught up in the mental health system. What possessed us to spend almost a decade in pursuit of the life stories of ordinary people who had died many years before, and whose stories would be told largely in our words and not theirs? Why piece together biographies from remnants when there are living people perfectly capable of telling their stories and having them recorded for posterity? A keenness to rummage through personal effects undisturbed by their owners was certainly a factor; another was the knowledge that these individuals never had the chance to tell their stories outside of the confines of psychiatry. What might be revealed by comparing the personal artifacts from their pre-institutional lives with the way they were perceived by doctors and hospital staff? Regardless of what might have troubled them, we were struck by the sundering of who they were as people from who they became as mental patients.

Psychiatry in those days (and still today) was largely in the business of stripping patients of their quotidian identities. Diagnostic categories serve mainly to pitch people into a few pigeonholes that help psychiatrists talk about them among themselves. This is not to say that nothing was ailing the people whose stories are featured here. Beyond their obvious physical complaints, they were sad, downtrodden, heartbroken, confused, distressed, angry, irritated—and irritating—fearful, convinced of being persecuted, troubled by voices of unseen speakers, soothed by visions of a celestial kind, shaken by religious fevers, in pain from loneliness, isolation, excessive excitement, and misguided love. Each one of them could be assigned one label or another, but none of these labels—schizophrenia, dementia praecox, melancholia, paranoia, manic-depression, delusional disorder—speaks to the narratives of their lives or gives color to their own unmistakable forms of suffering. Neither could those diagnostic categories, then or now, provide a basis for successful treatment and recovery. If anything, they stand in the way of healing, paths to which are suggested by the individual narratives.

If someone had taken the time and effort to piece together these people's stories during their lifetimes, a deeper understanding of their life circumstances might have led to a successful resumption of the lives they led before being institutionalized. Clearly, even with the best efforts, some people remain trapped in a web of misperception, fear, and self-loathing. Some of the suitcase owners might have remained forever distressed and unable to fully engage in society even if they had been afforded the best treatment. But then again, even they would certainly have done better if they had been treated with kindness and persistent care, and been given a chance to live in the outside world.

1.
HE TOOK THEM ON THEIR LAST WALK

For more than thirty years, a small man wearing heavy rubber boots strode around Willard State Hospital with a self-contained air and a general sense of industriousness. He was a well-known personage among the staff and patients. He expected to get his way, and, according to some workers who knew him, he usually did. A former director of nursing at Willard said, "He had seniority over the employees, the patients and everybody else." A retired nurse called him an "established member of the hospital." He wasn't the superintendent or a member of the medical staff; he was Lawrence Marek, a patient, and the institution's unpaid grave digger until the day he died at ninety years of age.

From 1937 until his death in 1968, Mr. Marek worked nearly every day in the patient cemetery, in every kind of weather, digging graves by hand and maintaining the expansive grounds overlooking Seneca Lake. Halfway up the gently rising slope of the thirty-acre burial ground, he built himself a simple wooden shack where he stayed during the warmer months of the year. A physician noted in his record, "He is happy, has found a home at the hospital." Perhaps that overstates the case, but certainly Lawrence figured out a way to make the best of the bad circumstances in which he found himself,

Lawrence's shack and Civil War graves, Willard Cemetery, c. 1960

and he built a life (of sorts) for himself while institutionalized for 52 years. Unlike most of the suitcase owners, Marek was able to find a sense of purpose within the restricted world of the hospital, a job that he took seriously and around which he built his identity, gaining a measure of local prestige and personal satisfaction.

> JANUARY 19, 1965: *Patient continues to be the well liked, hard working, quite original old man, walking with his 87 years in rain or snow every day to his job in the cemetery. He is always very pleasant and friendly, and possibly because of language difficulties mainly, not associating with others. He is always cheerful, playing his harmonica, however, mostly for himself in his shanty. Physically the patient is in excellent health for his age. Blood pressure 120/60. Medication: None.* —Adolph Hug, M.D.

Lawrence, by all accounts, was a master of his trade. "I remember that he could dig a grave that was almost perfectly . . . as a matter of fact, it looked like it *was* perfectly rectangular," former nursing director Laverne Dratt recalled. "I know that he had a wooden form that he laid down on the top so that he got it started. But I don't have any idea how you could possibly dig a hole in the ground six feet deep that was that perfect. . . . He used to wear hip waders when he was digging the grave, because often while he was digging, the water was seeping in. . . . And when he wasn't digging graves, he also wore the hip waders." He was meticulous, according to another former nursing director, Web Rankin: "I remember going over and seeing the grave and being impressed by his attention to the details of the burial and the fact that the cemetery was well-maintained. He was very fussy about it. His cemetery had to be properly maintained and he saw to it that it *was* maintained." Lawrence also made some pocket money by wrapping the bodies of his deceased fellow patients, according to Dratt. Preparing bodies for burial was the responsibility of the ward attendants, but they often avoided this unpleasant task by paying Marek a dollar or two to relieve them of this burden.

By taking on such grim but vital work that no one else wanted to do, Lawrence made himself indispensable to the hospital, which allowed him to take some liberties within the institutional regimen. "He didn't countenance any direction from other people. If the boss told him something, then he would. But if you were just a regular employee, he just kind of went his own way," Laverne Dratt said. His behavior, one doctor noted somewhat cryptically in the record, was "not in complete agreement with the rules, without causing any major difficulties." Among the rules Lawrence stretched was a strict policy that patients would be served only at regular mealtimes. "He used to go to the main kitchen; he was a patient who had special privileges. And [the kitchen staff] would feed him pretty much regardless of what time it was," according to Dratt.

A Self-sufficient Enclave

From its founding in 1869 until the latter part of the twentieth century, Willard, like other state-run mental institutions, was dependent upon unpaid patient labor to sustain its operations. The facility had over six hundred acres of farmland, with a greenhouse, a dairy, stables, chicken houses, piggeries, and barns where nearly all of the facility's food was raised and processed. There were industrial shops producing clothing and shoes, baskets and brooms, and other necessities such as soap, as well as huge laundries, bakeries, and kitchens. The hospital had a slaughterhouse, woodworking shops, brickworks, a blacksmith's shop, and a coal-fired power plant whose boilers were fed by patients hauling coal by wheelbarrow from the hospital's rail yard. These facilities were overseen by paid staff, but most of the work was done by patients, who also labored on the grounds crews, did the excavation for new construction, cleaned the wards and offices, served the food, and staffed the opulent home of the superintendent. In addition to Lawrence's work digging graves and tending the cemetery, patient laborers built the pine caskets and forged the numbered cast-iron grave markers used in lieu of gravestones.

This reliance on unpaid patient labor grew out of the philosophy that underlay the rapid expansion of state "lunatic asylums" in America in the latter half of the nineteenth century. Called moral treatment, this practice was developed by English Quakers in response to horrific conditions in overcrowded British madhouses during the Industrial Revolution. It was based on the belief that people newly diagnosed as mad could be cured by a firm but humane hand, a safe haven from the stresses of urban life, regular work, and rigorous instruction in small country asylums.

Importing moral treatment across the Atlantic resulted in certain American innovations that undermined the British Quakers' vision of small bucolic retreats where people would recover through nature, work, and education. American institutions were built to accommodate thousands of patients. Keeping the focus on labor, these asylums were designed as small cities with ample work for asylum inmates. Besides being seen as central to recovery, patient work was necessary for these huge institutions to sustain themselves without an excessive burden on taxpayers.

Large numbers of unpaid patient workers were particularly crucial at Willard, which was founded at the urging of one Dr. John Chapin for the express purpose of providing a final resting stop for "incurables." Chapin won the argument for such a massive facility by promising that it would be run far more cheaply than New York State's first asylum for acute cases at Utica, because it would rely more heavily on patient labor while curtailing the creature comforts afforded to those hopeless patients. Chapin was true to his word: during the years he managed Willard, the annual per-patient cost was only a third of that at Utica. For more than a hundred years, Willard remained nearly self-sufficient, sustained by the labor of its mostly unwilling charges. When unpaid patient labor was finally outlawed in New York in 1973, after more than a century of exploitation, this became a major factor in the exodus of patients from state hospitals that became known as deinstitutionalization. Without free labor, these huge institutions were simply unworkable.

Like many of his fellow patients who were good workers, Lawrence's industriousness made him so valuable to the institution that he was kept there long after he stopped experiencing any significant emotional distress.

HEARING THE ANGELS

The long and serpentine journey by which Lawrence Marek came to be an irreplaceable worker at Willard began in the village of Stultza Waerka in Austro-Hungarian Galicia, where he was born in 1878. Galicia was a remote and rural part of the empire. His father died when Lawrence was young, leaving his mother with five children to raise alone, and the family was dirt poor. Lawrence went to school for only three or four years. As a young man, he escaped this abject poverty by becoming a licensed itinerant tinker, collecting scrap and repairing metal objects throughout Austria and Germany. About 1900, three events irrevocably changed Marek's life: he received a head injury from a stone throw; he began drinking heavily; and he was admitted to the Grafenberg Asylum near Düsseldorf, Germany, for "singing, whistling, and (being) generally noisy." Alcohol was the precipitant for his behavior, which culminated in loud accusations against himself for having sinned, prostrating himself in an attitude of prayer. His first stay at an asylum lasted less than a year. In 1902, he joined the Kaiser's army, but no information was found about the nature or length of his service.

In 1907, at the age of twenty-nine, Lawrence immigrated to the United States, embarking from Hamburg on the *Kaiserin Augusta Victoria*. He passed through Ellis Island, in spite of his mental health history, and found work as a porter at the New York *Tribune* building on Park Row. Later he worked as a window washer at Bellevue Hospital, where he lived in a dormitory for single male workers.

Little is documented about Marek's life in New York before his 1916 admission to the psychiatric unit of Bellevue Hospital. Ironically, his place of employment became his downfall. During his admission interview, he told the doctor that he had taken classes at night school, but revealed little other information. His calfskin valise, bearing the initials L.M., held few clues about his former life.

    Suitcase—brown leather (soiled & deteriorating), leather handle, metal
        clasp closure
    Shoes—1 pair of men's black leather dress shoes; 3 button closure flap
    Mug, Shaving—blue w/black trim, blue side handle
    Mug, Shaving—white, bottom stamped in green print, "Chester Hotel China"
    Brush, Shaving—black knob handle w/metal shaft; bristles are yellowish
        and brittle
    Brush, Shaving—wood handle, metal shaft (broken); bristles are yellow-
        ish and brittle
    Suspenders—Heavy white elastic, soiled, button attachments

The record shows that after eleven apparently uneventful years as a cleaner and window washer in Manhattan, Lawrence caused a ruckus in the workers' dormitory at Bellevue, "singing and shouting and whistling in a boisterous manner." He was taken across the street to the hospital's alcoholic ward, and was transferred six days later to the psychiatric department. Chart entries state that he "was confused—depressed—had self accusatory ideas and continually assumed attitudes of prayer" and that "he must be urged to take nourishment—sleeps very poorly—requires medication and at times restraint—is very destructive and mischievous. At times he is flighty and elated. Again depressed and emotional."

From Bellevue, Marek was quickly sent to Central Islip State Hospital on Long Island, where the examining physician found that "he has for an undetermined period of time been hearing the voice of God and seeing visions of angels and other heavenly personages. He has numerous self-condemnatory ideas."

EXCERPTS FROM MENTAL STATUS EXAM CONDUCTED BY DR. H. ELKINS, JULY 31, 1916.

DR. H. ELKINS: How do you feel now?
LAWRENCE MAREK: Thank you, pretty good.
DR.: Do you feel happy?
LM: Yes.
DR.: Why do you feel so happy?
LM: God makes me so happy.
DR.: Did you ever see God?
LM: Sure.
DR.: What does he look like?
LM: I can't explain.
DR.: Where do you see God?
LM: In the church, anyplace. God is all over. God is talking to me now.
DR.: What does He say to you?
LM: Tell me not to do nothing wrong.
DR.: You don't always feel so happy. Sometimes you feel downhearted?
LM: It can't be helped.
DR.: What makes you downhearted?
LM: I done a whole lot of wrong things.
DR.: What did you do?
LM: I am ashamed to tell you.
DR.: What did you do?
LM: I was a liar the whole of my life.
DR.: What else?
LM: I killed flies. I didn't know it was a sin but it is.

DR.: Is that a crime, to kill flies?

LM: Yes. God says not to kill, not to kill anything.

DR.: You were sick once before?

LM: I was in Germany.

DR.: What was the matter with you in Germany?

LM: I was crazy. (*Smiles*)

DR.: You were crazy at that time?

LM: I really was.

DR.: But not now?

LM: No, I am not crazy now.

DR.: Your head is nice and clear?

LM: Yes, sir.

DR.: Do you sleep alright?

LM: I do.

DR.: Have any dreams now?

LM: I heard a nice song the last time.

DR.: Who sang the song?

LM: The angels.

DR.: Did you see the angels?

LM: No, I heard their voices.

Lawrence Marek appears to have been struggling with religious guilt and spiritual turmoil. Yet nowhere in his medical records is there any sign that doctors took his expressions of spiritual anguish seriously, or tried to determine the cause of his distress. His statements were attributed to hallucinations and their content dismissed as the ramblings of a madman; neither his old head injury nor his alcohol history figured into the doctors' diagnoses or treatment.

Throughout his two years at Central Islip, his behavior was somewhat erratic. Within two months of admission, he was described as "quiet and tractable. Has shown considerable improvement. He is anxious for his release." But a few weeks later, his behavior was reported as disruptive:

SEPTEMBER 23, 1916: *This noon, in the Dining Room, this patient suddenly became excited—he jumped up from his seat, threw over his chair, cleaned off the table, throwing the dishes around the room. It required the efforts of several attendants to restrain him, owing to his excited condition.*

By December of that year, he again showed "considerable improvement . . . [and] requested to be sent back to New York where he can get work and has several friends who will assist him to get employment." But his request for release was not granted. His condition continued to improve after he joined the grounds crew.

July 10, 1917: This patient has been employed for the past few months in out-door work, around the lawns and grounds, and has improved considerable as a result of the outdoor exercise. He is also much pleasanter and tractable. While in the ward he sits quietly in one place and has little to say to anyone.

In May 1918, Lawrence Marek was transferred to Willard, "one of a party of 25 men and 30 women accompanied by attendants and Dr. Elkins." Most likely, these people were transferred to make room for others in the overcrowded institutions near New York City.

For several years after he arrived at Willard, Lawrence tended to be volatile and occasionally attacked other patients when they bothered him; otherwise he was very reclusive. His condition was generally described as "dull and morose" or "unsocial, inclined to be uncommunicative" for the first twelve years he was there. He stayed on the ward much of the time, sometimes doing a bit of cleaning, but keeping mostly to himself.

REINVENTING HIMSELF THROUGH WORK

Throughout Marek's fifty years at Willard, his broken English and heavy accent often made conversation difficult. By the early 1930s, though, it became clear that he enjoyed physical labor and worked best when left to his own devices. In 1932, he became a cleaner in the superintendent's house, where he was observed talking "to imaginary voices which he calls devils." A few weeks later, the record noted that he was "a good ward worker, and goes out to do light work at different places about the institution . . . at present, is out picking peas." Over the next few years, he labored with the grounds crew, did painting and repairs, and was generally an industrious worker who preferred to spend his leisure time alone. During the 1930s, his religious concerns and any psychiatric symptoms were rarely mentioned in the record. By 1937, Marek had taken full responsibility for the patient graveyard. He seemed to thrive on the work of caring for the cemetery. Some years later, when his only coat was stolen, he sent this letter to Superintendent Dr. Kenneth Keill.

The letter was placed in his file to document what his doctors felt were irrational ideas. Dr. Keill did not respond to the letter, and Lawrence continued his work for another twenty-three years, apparently showing few signs of psychiatric problems. His medical record during that time tells a fairly consistent story:

APRIL 18, 1951: *Patient continues to work as the grave-digger on the cemetery. He is a bony, elderly man, still robust and in good physical health. He is quiet about the ward, and rather seclusive. He digged over 900 graves in 14 years, he said, and likes to be by himself.* —Dr. M. Jackamets

AUGUST 10, 1955: *This 77 year old white male patient is careless of his appearance but clean in his habits. He does not believe he is or ever was mentally ill. On the ward, the patient is rather seclusive. He has a parole card and works in the graveyard. He may be hallucinated but not to a marked degree. The patient is a well-developed and nourished white male, who appears much younger than his actual age.* —Dr. Waxman

JANUARY 16, 1961: *GOOD HEALTH, FAIRLY TIDY, COOPERATIVE, RELEVANT, LOGICAL, WELL ORIENTED, GOOD WORKER, MEMORY FAIRLY GOOD, JUDGEMENT AND INSIGHT FAIR. This is an elderly patient who is in good physical health. He is hard of hearing but works well. He doesn't consider himself mentally ill and denied hallucinations or delusions. He is fully oriented and gives good information about his life. He talks pleasantly and could carry on a conversation.* —Dr. Gungor

From the time he was fifty years old, and possibly even earlier, Lawrence rarely expressed any emotional distress. The religious guilt and turmoil he felt when he first entered the hospital apparently dissipated; perhaps he worked out his spiritual issues on his own, or maybe these concerns became secondary to the practical matters of survival in an institution. When neuroleptic drugs were first introduced to state mental hospitals in 1954, most patients were heavily medicated. Marck was not, and there is no indication that he received any psychiatric drugs during the rest of his life. Yet the issue of his release from Willard was not even broached in the medical record until he was in his mid-eighties.

NOVEMBER 18, 1963: *This 85 year old patient is an excellent worker in the cemetery. He has just grown old in this hospital. He has a heavy accent and, therefore, may be hard to understand at times. He, however, is fully oriented. He has no delusional trends and denies sense deceptions. He shows no psychopathology whatsoever but after 47 years of hospitalization, seems to have no other chance but to remain in the hospital and he actually does like it. General health is good. Medication: none.* —Dr. Hug

Dr. Hug's note documents what should have been obvious to the staff at Willard for decades: there was no valid reason to keep Lawrence Marek in a mental institution for more than two-thirds of his life. It seems ironic that his work, the one thing that gave him a sense of purpose during his years as a patient, was probably the main reason he remained at Willard for fifty years.

OCTOBER 16, 1968: PROGRESS NOTE
This 90 year old patient has been in this hospital since 1918 and had been treated for Schizophrenia: Paranoid Type. He has adjusted himself well to the hospital routine. He is cooperative and friendly to the nursing staff. He still makes a daily trip to the cemetery where he has worked for years. His physical condition appears to be satisfactory to his advanced age. He eats and sleeps well. Patient does not require any medication.
—*Quang-Hsi Hu, M.D.*

Two weeks after this note was written, Lawrence Marek died quietly in his sleep, and was buried in an anonymous numbered grave in the cemetery that he tended so dependably for so many years.

STATE HOSPITAL CEMETERIES TODAY:
A FOCAL POINT FOR ADVOCACY

By diligently preparing and maintaining the final resting places of his fellow patients, Mr. Marek was something of a pioneer. Across the United States, hundreds of thousands of state hospital patients were buried in anonymous numbered graves during the 19th and 20th centuries. These cemeteries are concrete reminders of the way patients were treated in death as well as in life. In some cases, they were buried only in shrouds, with no coffins or grave markers; in others, they were buried in pine boxes with small numbered markers. Some were cremated, and their ashes left in cans in storage sheds. The patients' remains were treated with the same lack of recognition and dignity that was their lot while they lived. Like the Willard suitcase owners, many spent decades in institutions, segregated from their communities, then died there, and were buried on the grounds, forgotten. Today, restoration of neglected state hospital cemeteries has become a focus of advocacy by former psychiatric patients and their allies, who want to restore dignity to the memories of those buried there, and to call attention to the still rampant prejudice and discrimination against people with psychiatric histories.

In 1997, ex-patient activist Patricia Deegan discovered a densely overgrown field full of numbered markers while walking her dog on the grounds of the now-closed Danvers State Hospital in Massachusetts. Realizing that she had stumbled upon patient graves, she was shocked by the fact that the graves bore no names and that the cemetery was not even minimally maintained. She photographed the markers and their neglected surroundings, began searching for cemetery records, and helped other ex-patients organize to demand that the Commonwealth restore the graveyards. "If people treat a cemetery like trash, it's a good indication of how they feel about the people buried there and those who are still receiving services," she said.

At meetings and conferences, Pat shared the existence of the Danvers cemeteries with other ex-patients around the country, inspiring them to find and restore abandoned burial grounds in their own communities. It turned out that there were hundreds of neglected state hospital cemeteries across the country, and many burial records were lost, incomplete, or declared off-limits because of "confidentiality" concerns. Only a handful of graves have headstones with the names of the deceased; some of these mark the graves of veterans, whose stones were paid for by the armed forces, while others were placed by family members. But most graves are marked only with numbers, if at all, and many of the markers were primitive. Some graves are marked by three-inch ceramic discs into which a number had been scratched, others by small granite squares. At Harlem Valley State Hospital in New York, hand-cut tin numbers were pressed into cement-filled coffee cans, while at Rockland State Hospital, numbered plates were fastened to cinder blocks. At New York's Kings Park State Hospital, a four-acre plot contains more than a thousand unmarked graves of nineteenth-century patients; their only identification: numbers written on slips of paper and put into glass bottles buried next to the shrouded bodies.

Conditions such as these resulted in dozens of cemetery restoration projects being organized in at least twenty states. Thousands of ex-patients and their allies became amateur historians, genealogists, and landscapers, working to identify unmarked graves and restore the cemetery grounds. Some state mental health authorities assisted the efforts with money or labor; a high-ranking mental health official in Georgia made a stirring public apology for the neglect of the cemeteries and for the continued neglect and abuse of patients. Ex-patients found that local civic groups, churches, and historical societies were often willing to join their restoration efforts. Working side by side with people who may never have knowingly met a former mental patient before, it became clear to ex-patients that the cemetery restoration effort served two purposes: it respectfully memorialized the long-forgotten patients who were buried anonymously, and it helped community members change some of their negative stereotypes about people with psychiatric histories. Pat Deegan explains the impact of the cemetery restoration efforts this way: "Cemetery restoration gave ex-patients and other activists a chance to take the moral high ground. We were seen as people who are able to make a positive contribution. And, as the effort caught on, it became a leadership development tool, as ex-patients learned how to organize and deal with the press. Finally, it gave many people a chance to grieve over what had happened to them. Often, their memories were so painful that they had never gone back to the state hospitals in which they had been housed."

At Willard, conditions at the cemetery slowly declined after Lawrence Marek's death in 1968. A small death benefit was made available to Medicare recipients, and more patients were buried in community cemeteries, while fewer were interred in the hospital cemetery. Except for the section containing the named stones of Civil War veterans who lived and died at Willard, graves were indicated by numbered rectangular cast-iron markers. The cemetery, which contains 5,776 graves, had its first burial in 1870, one year after the hospital opened. The last burial, in June 2000, was that of a former patient who died in a nursing home and asked to be buried at Willard.

During Lawrence's lifetime, roads were maintained throughout the cemetery, clearly distinguishing the separate sections set aside for people of various faiths. A map and index were available to locate a specific grave when family and friends came looking for their loved one's burial site. But sometime in the 1980s, the cast iron markers were removed to make mowing and maintenance easier, and most of the markers were tossed into the gully behind the cemetery hill. The roads were no longer kept up, and Lawrence Marek's meticulously manicured cemetery began to vanish. Willard's graveyard was not one of those that benefited from a restoration effort in recent years, and today it resembles a pasture.

Willard Cemetery, c. 1960

Willard Cemetery, 2000

2.
WHO WENT TO WILLARD AND WHY DID THEY GO THERE?

O n October 13, 1869, a steamboat docked at Ovid Landing on the eastern shore of Seneca Lake, and several men led a deformed woman down the gangplank: Mary Rote, Willard's first patient, had been chained for ten years without a bed or clothing in a cell in the Columbia County almshouse, 250 miles downriver.

Three more patients, men, arrived at the dock that day, all in irons, one in what looked like a chicken crate, three and a half feet square. By the end of 1870, the new institution housed 125 men and 450 women.

Many of Willard's early patients had been considered too difficult in respective poorhouses and had been subjected to regular floggings, dousing, and "pulleying" (hanging by the thumbs) in attempts to "quiet" them. The new asylum was founded as a destination for anyone considered incurably mad who was being held under less than ideal circumstances. America had woken up to the reality that people deemed mad were increasingly taking up space in poorhouses, jails, and cellars, and might be better served in a different kind of asylum. Following in the footsteps of French and British doctors like Philippe Pinel and William Tukes, who separated the mad from the Lumpenproletariat nearly fifty years earlier, American physicians like Sylvester Willard, for whom the institution was named, advocated for facilities that would serve precisely this purpose.

Unlike other state institutions that were set up to provide acute care to individuals from the surrounding communities, for its first twenty-five years, Willard received only patients from across the state who had already exhausted the public resources of their counties. Even paupers did not want to witness people kept in tiny cells and iron locks, being fed through openings in their doors, never let out until their limbs were crippled. Women were regularly abused by all comers, and the whole business had turned into a matter of public disgrace. Much better, it was reasoned, to ship people as far away as possible, sequestering them in a bucolic setting. There, they could be provided with an environment that was "morally" sound and designed to treat its charges through the strict but caring attitudes of their new keepers, under the guidance of medical personnel. But a selection took place even among the residents of poorhouses, since no one wanted to lose a worker who could be of help to their operation.

Mary Rote died of tuberculosis a few years after she arrived, but by 1877, Willard was filled with 1,550 people from all over the state. Nearly everyone who was admitted in the early days arrived by boat and left by hearse. Seneca Lake was a virtual River Lethe, but life inside the confines of Willard was said to be much improved compared to where its inmates came from. By the time Willard was converted from an "Asylum for the Insane" into a State Hospital in 1890, the railroad had replaced steamboat traffic, making the transfer of patients much more efficient. Being classified as a State Hospital meant that Willard was now open to both acute and chronic

Ferry Landing at Willard

"cases" from the surrounding eleven counties, but continued to receive the "hopeless" from other parts of the state as well. Before 1890, only individuals whose families or counties were willing to pay ended up in state asylums. After 1890, the state assumed the costs.

THEIR NUMBERS

Between its opening in 1869 and 1900, roughly 8,000 people entered Willard, of whom 1,500 (18 percent) were discharged as recovered, while the remainder eventually died there. Between 1900 and 1950, the patient census rose steadily, from 2,266 to 3,561, and in each year, many more patients died than were discharged. Of the 54,000 individuals who passed through Willard during its 126 years of operation, 5,776 are buried in the graveyard that was tended by Lawrence Marek. Another 18,000 died at the hospital of disease or old age, and most of them were buried by their families in their hometowns or by a local undertaker at a community cemetery in nearby Ovid. The bodies of others were donated to medical schools for scientific study. Nearly half the individuals who entered the sprawling facility left in a casket.

The population became older, too, over the life of the institution. In its last two decades, Willard was practically a geriatric facility, with the exception of acute admissions of younger patients from the surrounding counties.

After 1890, more patients came directly from their family homes and many were from better economic circumstances. Paupers were now mingling with better-situated citizens such as Josephine Smith, who in 1898 was sent to Willard by her family from Canandaigua when she suffered a second episode of depression. Five years earlier, they spent a small fortune having Josephine treated at the posh Long Island Home Hotel for Nervous Invalids in Amityville, whose residents were met at the train by a top-hatted driver, dined

Josephine Smith

with silver and fancy porcelain, and relaxed on Louis XV sofas in parlors. Apparently, such luxuriously appointed treatment had beneficial effects, since Josephine was returned in full recovery to her family home. When the money ran out and Josephine again showed signs of melancholy, the family money had run out and she was sent to Willard, where she spent the remaining seventy-five years of her life. She might have been the person with the longest continuous stay at Willard, dying there at the age of one hundred and one.

Along with Josephine, 128 men and 127 women were admitted to Willard in the year 1898/99. More than half came from their own homes, one-quarter from other state institutions, and only 13 from almshouses. Few were private payers and the vast majority were committed against their will. The demographic changes from the early pauper years to the last decade of the nineteenth century were quite dramatic: unlike the county charges sent to Willard between its opening day and its conversion to a State Hospital, the majority of the patients admitted after 1888 had at least graduated from common school. More than half were married, widowed, or divorced, and nearly all had worked in some capacity prior to their commitment. Some were obviously intellectuals, even bearing advanced degrees, while others were simple workers, laborers, chambermaids, or farmers. The work they did immediately preceding their commitment did not necessarily correspond with the social status of their origins. Quite a few of them came from the upper classes, but had descended into menial work, or even abject poverty and homelessness by the time they were sent to Willard.

THEIR OCCUPATIONS (1888-1900)*

Waiters, cooks, servants, etc. (Domestic service)	25%
Governesses, teachers, students, housekeepers, nurses	17%
Farmers, gardeners, herdsmen, etc.	14%
Laborers	13%
Blacksmiths, carpenters, engine fitters, sawyers, painters, police, etc.	8%
No occupation	6%
Bootmakers, bookbinders, compositors, weavers, tailors, bakers, etc.	3.2%
Tailoresses (*sic*), seamstresses, bookbinders, factory workers, etc.	2.3%
Unascertained	2%
Clergy, military and naval officers, physicians, lawyers, architects, artists, authors, civil engineers, surveyors (Professional)	< 2%
Miners, seamen, shopkeepers, saleswomen, stenographers, typewriters, prostitute (only one)	< 1% each

* *From the 32nd Annual Report of the Willard State Hospital, 1900.*

DURATION OF INSANITY PRIOR TO ADMISSION

Before 1900, Willard psychiatrists recorded the "duration of insanity" prior to admission; for 80 percent of new patients, this was less than six months. Today this would be considered a favorable prognostic sign, but back then, such a finding did not deter one from becoming a lifelong patient. Most individuals never left after their first admission to Willard, although, even then, doctors argued the earlier people came to the attention of psychiatry the greater their chances of recovery. Dr. Judson H. Andrews, assistant physician at Utica, wrote a paper—"Early Indications of Insanity"—suggesting that families take note of early signs such as "morbid dreams, sleep impairments, constant headaches, emotional exaggerations, excessive religious scruples, and changes in habits of dress and cleanliness."

GENDER

As noted earlier, by the end of its first year of operation, Willard housed four times as many women as men. Since most of these admissions came from poorhouses, perhaps county officials gave preference to women, who were more vulnerable to sexual assault. By 1900, the proportion of women and men admitted was equal. Women were more likely to be married than their male peers, but were twice as often widowed. Whether this was due to war or other calamities affecting men is hard to ascertain. Women were generally more vulnerable to long-term institutionalization because many were employed as domestics and in constant close contact with their employers. Any aberrant behavior or dispute with the employer could be construed as a sign of "mental illness" and result in commitment. More single women ended up at Willard, since other institutions preferably discharged single men, assuming that it would be easier for them to find work and social support. In the nineteenth century, many middle-class men sought to institutionalize their troublesome spouses with the help of male psychiatrists, who were all too willing to oblige.

ORIGINS

Early on, Willard had a significant proportion of foreign-born, Catholic, and especially Irish patients. In the nineteenth century, the Irish had fewer social resources than other foreign-born patients. They were more likely to be women, unskilled, and poorly educated. Only a minimal number of non-white patients came to Willard during the first fifty years of its operation. Until the mid-1920s, Native American and black patients were excluded in a discriminatory fashion due to the cost of state care. They continued to languish in almshouses or homeless encampments. Over the years, the ethnic composition of Willard's patients changed. African Americans arrived at Willard in increasing numbers, in proportion to their increase among the Northeast's general population and because of the relaxing of racist regulations.

The turn of the twentieth century and the aftermath of World War I brought a great influx of new immigrants. Between 1900 and 1918, almost 14.5 million people entered the United States, more than 95 percent of them through Ellis Island in New York Harbor. At Willard, the proportion of foreign-born patients kept inching up, as well as the number of those sent from hospitals in the New York City area. Until 1900, more than 30 percent of Willard patients were born in other countries, mostly Ireland, Germany, and England. The proportion of foreign-born patients increased until 1915, when it reached 36 percent, its highest mark. Correspondingly, the number of admissions from downstate areas, where most of the new immigrants resided, skyrocketed between 1900 and 1910, jumping from 7.5 percent in 1900 to 36 percent in 1926. In 1900 alone, 60 percent of all new admissions came from downstate counties. By the early 1950s, this trend had reversed, and only 2 out of 152 admissions came from New York City.

TABLE No. 2 — IN TWO PARTS — PART 1 — FIRST ADMISSIONS TO ANY HOSPITAL FOR INSANE — MEN.
October 1, 1907, to September 30, 1908

KEY a S.=Single; M.=Married; W.=Widowed. b N.=None. R.=Reads only. R. W.=Reads and writes. c* =A regular church attendant. D.=Divorced; SP.=Separated. C. S.=Common School. H. S.=High School; Col.=Collegiate. d C.=City; V.=Village; R.=Rural.

Clinical number	Nativity			Civil condition a	Education b	Occupation	Religion c	Residence d	Time in U. S.	Etiological factors other than heredity
	Patient	Father	Mother							
33180	N. Y.	N. Y.	N. Y.	W	C. S.	Farmer	Meth.*	V	......	Fract. skull.
29383	N. Y.	Eng.	Eng.	M	R. W	Farmer	Pres.*	R	......	Arterioscler, cer. haem.
29384	N. Y.	N. Y.	N. Y.	M	C. S.	Farmer	Meth.*	R	......	Cer. haem.
30815	N. Y.	N. Y.	N. Y.	M	C. S.	Carpenter	Prot.	C	......	Arterio scler.
31411	Scot.	Scot.	Scot.	M	Col	Clergyman	Bapt.*	V	19 yrs.	Cer. haem.
32555	Ire.	Ire.	Ire.	M	C. S.	Laborer	Meth.*	V	23 yrs.	Cer. haem.
35165	Ire.	Ire.	Ire.	M	C. S.	Fireman	R. C.*	V	40 yrs.	Cer. haem.
35725	N. Y.	N. Y.	N. Y.	M	C. S.	Night watchman	Prot	V	......	Alcoholism.
35722	N. Y.	N. Y.	N. Y.	S	H. S.	Night watchman	Bapt.	V	......	Chorea.
31400	N. Y.	N. Y.	N. Y.	W	C. S.	Advertising agent	Meth.*	C	......	Sexual excesses.
30005	N. Y.	N. Y.	N. Y.	W	C. S.	Farmer	Meth.*	R	......	Senility and cardiac dila.
30014	Ire.	Ire.	Ire.	W	N	Railroad laborer	R. C.*	V	56 yrs.	Arterio scler, senility.
30257	N. Y.	N. Y.	N. Y.	S	C. S.	None	Meth.	C	......	Senility.
30258	N. Y.	Pa.	Pa.	D	C. S.	Farmer	None	R	......	Senility and chr. endocarditis.
30267	Mass.	Mass.	Mass.	W	C. S.	Carpenter	Meth.*	R	......	Senility and loss of wife.
31408	N. Y.	N. Y.	N. Y.	M	C. S.	Blacksmith	None	V	......	Alcoholism and senility.
31901	Eng.	Eng.	Eng.	M	R. W	Laborer	Meth.	R	35 years.	Senility.
31908	Mass.	Mass.	Mass.	W	C. S.	Cabinet maker	Meth.	C	......	Senility.
32556	N. Y.	Eng.	Eng.	M	R. W	Carpenter	Pres.	C	......	Alcoholism, pneumonia.
33181	Eng.	Eng.	Eng.	W	C. S.	Spectacle maker	Epis.	C	40 years.	Senility.
33193	Ger.	Ger.	Ger.	M	R. W	Farmer	Chris.Church	R	72 years	Senility, cataract op.
33195	Mich.	N. Y.	N. Y.	M	C. S.	Farmer	R. C.*	R	......	Arterioscler, influenza.
35727	Ger.	Ger.	Ger.	M	C. S.	Shoemaker	R. C.*	V	60 years.	Senility.
35729	N. Y.	Ger.	Ger.	M	C. S.	None	None	C	......	Arterioscler.
29381	Pa.	N. J.	N. Y.	S	H. S.	Clerk	Bapt.*	C	......	Syphilis.
30012	Can.	Ire.	Can.	W	C. S.	Mach. shoe operator	Meth.	C	27 years.	Syphilis.
30020	Den.	Den.	Den.	S	C. S.	Telegraph operator	Meth.	O	10 years.	Syphilis and alcohol.
30024	Den.	Den.	Den.	S	C. S.	Fisherman	None	V	......	Alcohol.
32561	N. Y.	Eng.	N. Y.	D	C. S.	Auctioneer	None	V	......	Syphilis.

With immigration surging in the early 1900s and then abating during the Depression, the population of foreign-born residents at Willard gradually declined. Of our selected sample, the vast majority were born outside the United States: in Germany, the Philippines, Scotland, eastern Europe, France, and Egypt. This over-representation may reflect the fact that foreign-born, urban residents had fewer community connections than those coming from rural upstate areas, and thus brought more of their belongings to Willard. Of all the suitcase owners we studied, the ones who had more varied and colorful contents in their trunks were also the ones with the least viable connections to the outside world.

Many patients were sent to Willard from other state hospitals in Brooklyn, Manhattan, Long Island, Buffalo, and Rochester. They often arrived in groups of a hundred or more. Special trains (and later buses) were crammed with patients who generally did not know where they were being taken, and arrived at Willard bewildered and lost, occasionally trying to flee.

On February 18, 1919, sixty-five men and fifty-one women from Manhattan State Hospital arrived at Willard in the company of several attendants and one assistant physician, Dr. Audrey. Among them was Marie Lehner (Chapter 4), whose tattered doctor's bag was found in the Willard attic. Compared to a group that arrived around the same time from upstate areas, they were a bit younger (mean age 40 vs. 44.5) and, consequently, stayed longer at Willard. Their mean age at death was nearly identical, around 65, suggesting that institutional life affected all inmates about equally. A quarter of those who died were younger than 50, many due to outbreaks of infectious diseases like tuberculous, typhoid fever, cholera, and diphtheria. There were some, like 101-year-old Josephine Smith, who lived to a very old age at Willard, but this was the exception not the rule.

Since upstate people were more likely to come from family homes, it follows that they would have been kept there longer, even if they showed signs of disturbance. Downstate patients were much more likely to be single, foreign-born, and disaffiliated, and society did not afford them the same level of tolerance and support that their upstate peers had. The number discharged back to the community was negligibly small for both upstate and downstate patients, suggesting that institutional policies dictated the fate of these people, rather than any opportunities that may have been available to them outside the walls of Willard.

FAMILY RELATIONS

Many nineteenth century admissions were initiated by families after many years of tolerating problematic behavior, with wealthier families taking an even longer time to move towards commitment. Of the twenty-nine suitcase owners we initially selected for closer study, only eight came from their family homes and their families were involved in their commitment. Only one person came as a voluntary admission, and no one in our sample who was transferred from a downstate institution lived with a family member prior to admission. In fact, none of the people included in this book lived with their family prior to admission, or had family members involved in their commitment.

A majority of the suitcase owners had visitors during the first few years of their stay, but those visits became few and far between, as the visitors lost the enthusiasm for braving long distances and perennial disappointments. Families of immigrants who remained behind in the old country may not have even known that their relatives had been admitted. In the entire group of suitcase owners we studied, there were two divorcées, one widower, and one person in a long-standing intimate relationship. The others had never been married.

WHAT KIND OF PROBLEMS
BROUGHT PEOPLE TO WILLARD

The experiences and behaviors that caused someone to be sent to Willard ranged widely, from years of bothersome "agitation" that was used to justify solitary confinement and physical restraint, to minor social nuisances and the inability to secure work. Very few among the suitcase owners had a history of alleged violence against themselves or others. While some refused food because they suspected it might be poisoned, no one made an overt suicide attempt or an attempt on someone else's life. Frank Coles (Chapter 10), as far as we know, had only a single angry public outburst, for which he was arrested and transferred to a mental hospital, never to emerge. Dmytre Zarchuk was a law-abiding citizen detained by the Secret Service for appearing at the White House, seeking the hand of the president's daughter.

Violence or threats were more common among those suffering from neurological conditions that affected their behavior, such as neurosyphilis and other types of dementia. The proportion of such cases at Willard was high in its early years, because there was no treatment for these conditions, and there was a high frequency of disturbing behavior for which no other institutions were available at the time. Older people who showed signs of Alzheimer's-like dementia also had nowhere else to turn, as the case of Charles Farkas demonstrates. An eighty-four-year-old Jewish man, who had worked as a peddler on the Lower East Side before opening his own shoe store, found himself in a confused state, abandoned by his children. He ended up living in the Jamaica Railroad Station, eschewing his rented room only several blocks away. Railroad police intervened when the old man became a nuisance to them, and sent him before a judge, where he made the following statement:

> *I am 75 years old [sic]. I am here a week for nothing at all. I live in Jamaica. I went to the station house and they threw me out. I refused to go, so I spit on the floor, so they locked me up. I had a good name. I don't drink. I don't gamble. I got no place to go. I was a wealthy man. I am 50 years in America. I got the citizen papers home. I can bring it to you. I get $43 a month from the government. . . . I don't know where my wife is. I gave her a divorce. I was told she is in Florida. I have one son. I think he is in the army. I hear voices all day long. I can't understand what they say. They told me to sprinkle alcohol. I did but it didn't help. I sleep about two hours a day. No, I don't have any friends.*

When his daughter learned that her father had been taken to a mental institution hundreds of miles north, she could do little more than send him a few items and pay for his funeral four years later. In his large steamer trunk, we found a pair of well-used phylacteries and prayer books, fancy shoes, and galoshes—the accoutrements of a reasonably well-off Jewish man from New York's Lower East Side.

It is hard to know how many people experienced physical or emotional abuse or other serious trauma prior to becoming psychiatric patients A few of the suitcase owners offer hints of such events, which have been identified in recent years as important precursors to many psychiatric conditions. Margaret Dunleavy experienced the death of both parents and placement in an orphanage before the age of ten. Dmytre Zarchuk endured slave labor under the Nazis and the death of his wife and unborn child. Ethel Smalls was certainly beaten by her drunkard husband and traumatized by losing two of her children. The information about others is too sketchy to conclude whether they had experienced sexual or physical abuse or other trauma. Most likely they were never asked about it. When psychiatrists referred to "sexual abuse" in those days, they generally meant "self-abuse"—that is, excessive masturbation.

Prior to the late nineteenth century, homosexuality was seen primarily as a sin or a crime. But Victorian psychiatrists tried to bring what they considered a more "scientific" view of human behavior to the issue, and homosexuality was considered a "mental illness" until 1973, when the American Psychiatric Association removed it from its list of diagnoses. By the time Willard opened, most psychiatrists believed that men were biologically aggressive and women biologically passive, and that people who diverged from their expected gender roles or who were attracted to their own gender had an illness. While early Willard records do not list homosexuality as a cause of madness among those admitted, the case of Lucy Ann Lobdell, committed to Willard in 1880, demonstrates the clinical attitudes of the time. As described by Lynn Gamwell and Nancy Tomes in their book *Madness in America,* when she was abandoned by her husband at age seventeen, Lucy "donned male apparel and adopted the life of a hunter." She supported herself this way for about twenty years, and in 1868 began a relationship with another abandoned wife. The two lived for several years in the wilderness, sleeping in caves and surviving on game and berries. Eventually, they were jailed as paupers, and when it was discovered that "Mr. Lobdell" was really a woman, Lucy was sent to Willard. The reasons for her commitment included that "she insists on wearing male apparel" and "she calls herself a huntress." She was transferred to Binghamton State Hospital in 1892, where she died in 1912 at the age of eighty-three.

Another common pathway to the asylum that virtually guaranteed lifelong institutionalization was a diagnosis of "schizophrenia" or "dementia praecox," as this mysterious and mystifying condition was known at Willard well into the 1950s. In 1951, 56 percent of the 3,272 inpatients carried this diagnosis. In contrast, manic depression was only diagnosed in 4 percent of inpatients, whereas in 1900, mania and melancholia accounted for 34 percent of the population, and dementia praecox did not appear at all. In the late nineteenth century, psychiatrists favored a very broad approach to diagnostic categories that merited institutional treatment. As Ellen Dwyer put it in *Homes for the Mad: Life Inside Two Nineteenth Century Asylums*: "Almost every form of neurotic disorder that affects the moral powers in any way" justified admission to an asylum. Emphasis was placed on eccentric behavior that represented a shift from previous patterns. "The quiet had become noisy and the loquacious quiet; the industrious had given up their work, and agnostics had become religious fanatics; the virtuous suddenly showed signs of promiscuity." As Elaine Showalter wrote in *Victorian Woman and Insanity.* "Madness was no longer a gross and unmistakable inversion of appropriate conduct, but a collection of cumulatively disquieting gestures and postures."

And yet dementia praecox (later called schizophrenia) was the most common diagnosis on the admission papers of patients arriving at Willard, as it continues to be today. Even from this extremely cursory historical account, it becomes clear that psychiatrists did not know what to do with the majority of their patients, giving them varying and often contradictory diagnoses over the years. These diagnoses described little and explained even less. It goes beyond the scope of this book to fully discuss the issues associated with psychiatric diagnostics in general. Willard, like most mainstream psychiatric institutions, was subject to the rise of biological reductionism in psychiatry that began in the early twentieth century. Only a small number of diagnoses like schizophrenia and manic-depressive illness were used to classify patients, in the hope of finding biological mechanisms that would unlock their mysterious origins.

In the early days of Willard, medical perspectives about the origins of madness were still open to possible causes other than brain pathology. Emotional and economic stress were seen as perfectly acceptable causes for mental disturbance, as were more abstruse ideas such as excessive masturbation ("sexual abuse") and general lewdness. Heredity played a rather minor role, based on careful family histories, while neurological and other physical causes were well represented among Willard patients. The interface between medical illness and psychiatric symptoms is still poorly understood to this day, but this was a fairly frequent occurrence among Willard patients. Margaret Dunleavy (Chapter 6) and Ethel Smalls (Chapter 5) are prime examples of such "co-morbidity" and the largely unexplored forces that are apt to cross the boundaries between pain caused by ulcers, ulcers caused by mental distress, and mental distress caused by gastrointestinal problems. But there were many others. Not a few Willard patients, mostly men, were considered "intemperate"; in other words, they would be seen today as alcoholics. Intemperance was not considered an addictive disorder, but a kind of moral flaw, a lack of control or inhibition, possibly rectifiable by moral or religious intercession.

Classification according to diagnosis became a moot point when people entered Willard, due to the fact that they were entirely categorized according to their "manageability" and willingness to work. Whatever they may have been suffering from earlier was seemingly considered irrelevant the minute they were admitted to a psychiatric institution that was ostensibly set up for their treatment. No one would suggest that the individuals featured in this book, and the many thousands of others who joined them at Willard over the years, were fully integrated, well adjusted citizens enjoying wholesome lives before their incarceration. They indeed had many problems, frequently of social origin, sometimes set off by alcohol use, family conflict, trauma, abandonment, loss of work, poverty, and so forth. In some instances, a mysterious transformation seemed to take place, where people experienced disconcerting voices, became increasingly fearful and mistrusting of others, and sank into a melancholic state and could no longer care for themselves. These experiences, in psychiatric parlance referred to as "hallucinations," "paranoia," and "major depression," are not, as commonly suggested, indications of a chemical alteration in the brain. They are instead human responses to stress and adversity that fall outside the realm of the acceptable in broader society.

It is easy to understand fear, anxiety, aggression, even suicidal tendencies, but it is harder to fathom why someone might be hearing critical voices in the absence of anyone in the room, or why someone would consistently read adverse intentions into mundane signs such as TV programs or newsprint. It is also true that these experiences can occur with clear-cut neurological conditions, such as Alzheimer's dementia, multiple sclerosis, Wilson's disease, and others. This promotes an association with brain disease for all these unfamiliar and disconcerting experiences, rather than a conclusion that they are merely infrequent and unusual manifestations of human psychological response. Nearly 5 percent of the general population hears disembodied voices without ever consulting a psychiatrist. Millions are by nature suspicious and under certain circumstances become convinced that they are subject of nefarious, rather unlikely plots. This supports the notion of a continuum of human experiences, rather than a categorical distinction between normality and "mental illness." It seems clear that any psychiatric diagnosis assigned to the individuals featured here by their doctors did not contribute to their recovery, and instead sealed their fate as lifelong mental patients. Anything that would have been relevant to their recovery was buried beneath these diagnoses. In this book, we attempt to reveal these factors to the extent possible, recognizing that these people are no longer here to explain themselves.

The vast majority of the people who came through Willard died along with their stories. Whatever was entered in their medical records is irretrievably sealed, only accessible to research studies that disguise the identity and the particulars of their subjects. As much as the treasure of materials found in the suitcases allows us to delve into the life stories of a tiny segment of Willard's population, it casts an even larger shadow on the thousands of stories that will remain lost forever. This phenomenon occurs in all instances when particular details are learned about individuals who passed through tragedy, who died in wars, were exterminated in concentration camps, or went through slavery or other devastation. Knowing something about a few people makes us yearn to learn more about the many thousands, even millions, which these few represent. But there is a risk of false generalization and, in the case of a mental institution, generalizations may be even more problematic than for other human calamities. When considering wars or famines, we must assume that no one deserved to have gone through these experiences (unless, of course, they were perpetrators). But a mental institution is supposed to be a place of healing and support. People sometimes go there voluntarily, and some do get better at times, return to their previous lives, and occasionally even advance in their careers, start families, and rejoin their communities. But as the suitcase owners' lives show, many do not find healing, and the treatment can be spirit-breaking.

3.
HOW I WOULD HAVE FURNISHED MY ROOM (IF NOT FOR THE VOICES)

*"We came to this country to conduct our-
selves as free men."*
*—from a published letter to the editor of
the* Herald-Republican *by Rodrigo Lagon*

Mrs. Louise Maycock, the wife of a prominent Buffalo doctor, went before a judge in September 1917 seeking to have her house servant committed to a mental hospital. "The patient has been in my employ for the past two months. During the past month he has been very depressed, complaining of many and various pains, he now believes that spirits are constantly talking to him telling him that he has sinned and must confess to a priest," she testified. The judge signed the papers, and Rodrigo Lagon, a young Filipino man who was sent by his family to study in America, was remanded to Buffalo State Hospital, beginning a sixty-four-year confinement. Two years later, he was transferred to Willard. Mrs. Maycock's use of the word *patient* is telling: she apparently believed that the outcome of the proceedings was a foregone conclusion, given that she was the wife of a doctor and he was a homeless Asian man.

"MY SCHOOL MEMORIES IN AMERICA"

Rodrigo Lagon, a native of Mambusao in the Philippine Islands' province of Capiz, came from a prominent family of bankers and politicians, as evidenced by newspaper clippings and letters found in his trunk. He arrived in Salt Lake City, Utah, in 1907, as a third-grade elementary school student. As a youth, he was a passionate advocate for Philippine independence from the United States, writing letters to newspapers, helping to organize Filipino-American groups, attending rallies, and subscribing to pro-independence journals. Why he ended up as a house servant in Buffalo ten years after he arrived in the United States is a mystery. His writings describe parts of his life in America, but nothing explains how such an earnest and promising young student became a domestic, then went on to spend his entire adult life in a mental institution so far from home. At some point he must have fallen off the track that would have led to a government or military career, but the evidence left behind does not fully explain when or why.

A handwritten manuscript entitled "My School Memories in America—With Photographs" emerged from his trunk. He wrote it in 1919, just around the time he was sent to Willard. The photographs are missing and the document ends mid-sentence, but it contains his description of the four schools he attended in Salt Lake City, with each building and its exact location, the subjects he studied, and mention of his relationships with some of his classmates.

15902.55 SMALL BOOKLET, BLUE MARBLEIZED PAPER AND TWO WHITE SHEETS FOLDED IN HALF INSIDE, 12 PAGES HAND WRITTEN IN PENCIL ON LINED PAPER. (EXCERPT)

As a Pupil of the Wasitch Public School, Salt Lake City, Utah
Early in the Autumn of the year 1907 I became a pupil of this school. This beautiful large brick school is located near South Temple Street on R Street which a year after, its name was changed to Elizabeth Street. At this school I studied the following: English Grammar, Arithmetic, Geography, Hygiene, Music, Spelling, Physical Culture and Carpentry. Here I obtained some knowledge about the works of Henry W. Longfellow and learned by heart the immortal speech of Abraham Lincoln, "The Gettysburg Speech." The stage coach wagon which belongs to the fort used to carry us down to school. Here were five oriental students attending including myself: Sixto B. Cedilla, a countryman of mine, and others native of Corea. I became acquainted with them while a pupil in this school.

Rodrigo completed sixth grade at Wasitch in 1910, took his seventh-grade courses at a YMCA summer school, and entered the Bryant Preparatory School that fall, from which he graduated in 1911. "One of my happiest

Bryant Preparatory Academy 8th grade graduation, Salt Lake City, 1911

and pleasant days was when a photographer gave us a snap of his camera in front of the school building in that beautiful but memorable summer morning, and far happier and prouder when my name was called to present me my school certificate," he wrote about his eighth-grade graduation day. He added that he brought the certificate home to show his minister, who "was delighted and felt proud."

The fact that he shared his graduation happiness with his pastor and probably not with his family raises questions about why he came to the United States in the first place and what kind of relationship, if any, he maintained with his family. Only tentative answers can be found in the many letters and photographs from his trunk and in notes from his hospital record. Distant as he was from his parents, we would have expected an exchange of letters, but none were found. He was obviously close to his pastor, the Reverend Short, might even have boarded with his family, and kept in touch with him throughout the years.

It was unusual for a boy like Rodrigo to come to America from the Philippines by himself. In 1896, long-smoldering opposition to more than 350 years of Spanish occupation led to a popular insurrection when a brilliant Filipino physician, artist, writer, and pro-independence political thinker, Dr. José Rizal, was executed by Spanish authorities after a show trial on trumped-up charges. In 1898, the Philippines declared its independence from

Spain, and a republic was instituted. That same year, the Treaty of Paris ended the Spanish-American War, and Spain ceded the Philippines to the United States. President William McKinley proposed a "benevolent assimilation" of the Philippines as a U.S. colonial territory, an idea that was rather unpopular in the newly independent nation. This resulted in a four-year war between the United States and the Philippines, during which the Philippine president was captured and forced to issue a proclamation of surrender, ending the republic. A new government was set up, nominally run by Filipinos but ultimately controlled by the United States. At least two of Rodrigo's uncles were ministers in this government. Obviously, some members of Rodrigo's family were on the American side, favoring a quasi-colonial relationship.

Wary of the Filipino's strong desire for independence, the U.S. occupiers set out to cultivate good relations with the Filipino elite who had prospered under Spanish rule. Among their tactics was a program begun in 1903 that paid for a small number of children of the wealthy to attend college in the United States. The hope was that these *pensionados*, as they were called, would become Westernized and return to the Philippines to work as civil servants under U.S. rule. But Rodrigo, just an elementary school student, was certainly not a *pensionado*, so his way must have been paid by his family or perhaps by a missionary group, since his family had converted to Protestantism. At some point during his long hospitalization Lagon stated that an officer brought him to this country from the Philippines in 1907. We do not know whether such an officer ever existed, but in some ways Rodrigo Lagon was on an official mission in America, aborted by voice-hearing and perpetual incarceration.

Unanswered, too, is the question of Rodrigo's relationship with his parents. His trunk contains letters from uncles and cousins, as well as drafts of some of Rodrigo's letters to them, but no correspondence with his parents. He never mentions them in any of his letters to other family members. A cousin writes that Rodrigo's mother was anxious to see photographs of her son in the United States, which is the only reference to his parents among all his personal papers. His parents' names are listed on a statistical data sheet in his hospital record, with the word *insane* entered next to his father's name.

Rodrigo's grades proved him to be an industrious student who performed well above the average, especially for someone for whom English was not his first language. After graduating from the Bryant Preparatory School, he entered Salt Lake High School in 1911, and studied there at least through 1912. But soon thereafter Lagon moved to Chicago and enrolled in Wendell Phillips High School. In 1913, this was a racially mixed school that became Chicago's first predominantly African American high school. Maybe he felt shunned as a minority student in the lily-white schools of Salt Lake City and found refuge in the integrated urbanity of Chicago. Possibly, he was even treated as Chinese or Japanese, both much hated minority groups in Utah around the turn of the century. Much later he said that he "came to America, completed two years of high school, and then 'ran away.'" If so, why, and from whom, we really do not know.

15902.247 CLASS ASSIGNMENT ENGLISH COMPOSITION, ONE PAGE, "HOW I WOULD LIKE TO FURNISH MY ROOM," GRADE ON BACK: "B"

I would like to furnish my room with one table, two chairs one of which is a rocking chair a dresser and a closet. It must be well ventilated and lighted. I shall decorate my room with the pennants of the schools I have attended, such as the Wasatch School where I graduated (pink & white), the Salt Lake High School (red and black) and the Wendell Phillips High School. I shall also hang the picture of Dr. José Rizal, "The Founder of Our Fatherland," the picture of Hon. Emilio Aquinaldo, the ex-president of our past Republic, the picture of Apolinario Mabini, who was the wisdom of the Revolution and the First Premier of the Government of the Philippines and last of all the picture of Sir Galahad, the hero in King Arthur's Round Table. These pictures are very good and I love them with all my heart.—R. L .

The fact that Rodrigo venerated Rizal, a martyr for Filipino independence; Aquinaldo, who led the rebellious charge against the American puppet government; and Mabini, who was captured and exiled by the Americans, puts him squarely against the interests of his family, at least some of whom cooperated with the occupying American forces.

In another ironic twist for a boy who was obviously against the American military occupation of his country, in 1914, Rodrigo served as a wardroom boy aboard an Illinois Naval Reserve ship patrolling the Great Lakes. The captain gave him a good letter of recommendation and his fanciful cap ended up in his Willard trunk, along with photographs showing him on the ship with the crew, and a color postcard of Mackinac Island,

Rodrigo and Illinois Naval Reserve crew, Lake Michigan, 1914

Michigan. "This picture was taken at McKinac [*sic*] Island during summer time" was written in pencil on the back of one of the pictures.

> 15902.228 *Cap, sailor type, navy blue wool cap with two light blue stripes around band, black coated leather band and brim, gold embossed with eagle with shield on crest and sun above buttons, leather head band, black cotton lining, label in center cap lining "The Henderson Ames Co/ Kalamazoo, Mich" written under griffins on either side of a shield with crown on the top. This cap may have been part of the uniform worn while serving on ship around Mackinac Island. Photos (15902.208, 209) show in white caps. This may have been part of a dress uniform.*

Whatever brought him to Chicago from Salt Lake City, Rodrigo Lagon found companionship and common purpose among a group of young Filipino men and was active in the Filipino Association of Chicago. He was probably involved with its founding; a rough draft of the organization's by-laws in his handwriting was found in his trunk. He was also a member of the Methodist church, and at one time seriously considered studying for the ministry. He became friendly with Mr. and Mrs. Charles Weber Henson, church members who extended themselves to foreign students, holding dinners and Bible study classes at their home. Mrs. Henson assisted Rodrigo with his writing, and kept in touch with him during his first few years of hospitalization. Among his papers were invitations to formal events from the Filipino community in Chicago, some of which he received after he became a patient at Willard.

Through the church, Rodrigo also met a young woman in whom he took a romantic interest. His essay "The True Meaning of Christmas" is "lovingly dedicated to Miss Grace A. Smith"; another essay was also dedicated to Grace, but her name was lightly crossed out and replaced by the inscription "my wife." He also authored several poems with longing references to this woman, poems that were probably written during his hospital stay. No letters between the couple were found, so to what extent she returned his devotion is unknown. But Rodrigo wrote a novella with obvious autobiographical underpinnings, in which a young Filipino man is in love with an American girl. The girl's widowed mother, whose husband died fighting in the Philippines, disapproves of the relationship and works frantically and effectively to keep the lovers apart.

Sometime in 1916, Rodrigo Lagon left Chicago and moved to Buffalo, apparently without graduating from Wendell Phillips High School; he was eighteen years old. Letters from Mrs. Henson drop hints that perhaps Grace Smith moved to Buffalo and Rodrigo followed her. A letter dated July 1917 somewhat cryptically states, "No reason why I should say anything about Grace to the boys," while a letter in August says that Mrs. Henson has enclosed "a little medicine, when taken will help brace you for your talk with Grace—a harmless nerve tonic, let me know and will send more." So it seems that just as he began expressing the feelings of depression that soon landed him in Buffalo State Hospital, Rodrigo was steeling himself for an important conversation with Grace, one that apparently did not go well. On his admission to Buffalo, he was found to have syphilis, and perhaps this was what he dreaded telling Grace. Whatever the conversation entailed, it apparently put an end to any hope he had of marrying her.

ANNOYED BY THE VOICES

> *"Voices might be a problem, but not every problem is an illness."*
>
> —SANDRA ESCHER, *psychiatric researcher*

The fact that Rodrigo Lagon reported hearing voices telling him that he had sinned was almost certainly the reason for the judge's decision to certify his commitment. Auditory hallucinations, as the phenomenon of hearing voices is labeled in clinical terms, have long been identified by psychiatry as a first-rank symptom of the disorder called schizophrenia. Yet there is a growing body of research, conducted primarily in Europe since the 1980s, showing that many people hear voices but never come to the attention of mental health authorities. "Hearing voices in itself is not a symptom of an illness, but is apparent in 2–3% of the population. One in three becomes a psychiatric patient—but two in three can cope well," according to Marius Romme, emeritus professor at the University of Maastricht in The Netherlands, and one of the key researchers in this area. "The difference between patients hearing voices, and non-patients hearing voices, is their relationship with the voices. Those who never became patients accepted their voices and use them as advisers." Romme concluded that since so many people who heard voices were successfully integrated into their communities and did not find the voices problematic, voice-hearing in and of itself does not need to result in disability: "When you identify hearing voices with illness and try to kill the voices with neuroleptic medication, you just miss the personal problems that lay at the roots of hearing voices—and you will not help the person solving those problems. You just make a chronic patient."

In a study comparing the experiences of non-patient voice-hearers and those who became psychiatric patients, Dr. Adrain Honig of the University of Maastricht and his colleagues found that those in the patient group were more frightened of the voices, felt they had less control over them, and that the messages of their voices were more malevolent. Other researchers have found that psychiatric drugs are only effective in stopping the voices for about 35 percent of people who are given such drugs for this purpose. The research conducted by Romme and science journalist and research fellow Sandra Escher showed that 70 percent of people who hear voices report that the voices began after a traumatic or intensely emotional event.

Rodrigo's voices, which began shortly after the fateful meeting with his beloved Grace Smith, were negative and condemnatory. According to a 1935 note in his record, "he has been annoyed by the voices for 12 years now and since he has been very patient with them he thinks they should stop their torturing him and allow him to return to his studies." But the harsh, critical voices continued for decades, and he did the best he could on his own to minimize their negative impact.

JANUARY 30, 1930: *This patient has ground parole, has very active hallucinations of hearing. When he is hallucinated, he tells the charge of the ward and he asks to be kept in because he is afraid to go out. He is oriented as to time, place and person. Has some insight into his condition.*
—E.D.K.

If Rodrigo Lagon were alive today and fortunate enough to live in Great Britain, Scandinavia, or The Netherlands, he would have the opportunity to join a group of fellow voice-hearers who gather to provide mutual support for exploring the meaning of the voices and for coping successfully with negative voices. There is now an international network of hearing voices groups, which are user-run alternatives to the traditional psychiatric interventions for voice-hearing. Many in the Hearing Voices Network believe that the voices "are similar to dreams, symbols of our unconscious minds. Although the Network is open to many diverse opinions, we accept the explanation of each individual voice hearer." Among the network's goals is to provide a safe haven for voice-hearers to explore their experiences in a non-judgmental environment and to help people discover ways in which they can learn to live with the voices and regain control over their lives. Perhaps because of the powerful influence of pharmaceutical manufacturers on psychiatric practice in the United States, the Hearing Voices Movement has not yet made much headway here, although there is interest among ex-patient groups, who feel that many could benefit by having this option available.

Mr. Lagon's only recourse against the voices was to stay inside and accept the protection of the hospital. No other help was ever offered to him. Apparently, no one spoke to him about these voices at length, nor offered him strategies to distract himself or to suppress the voices.

"I HAVE NO DEFINITE KNOWLEDGE YET OF WHEN I SHALL REGAIN MY FREEDOM"

Despite the voices, Lagon maintained an active interest in the Filipino independence movement, subscribing to several related publications and carrying on correspondence with other activists, at least during the first few years of his institutionalization. Many publications, letters, and clippings about the situation in the Philippines dating from the 1920s somehow ended up in his trunk, maybe culled from the materials he was allowed to keep on the ward, maybe occasioned by a transfer to a more restrictive environment. A newspaper article about the Adirondacks from 1920 bears the penciled notation "Property of R. D. L-/ to be placed in my trunk."

15902.15 DRAFT OF LETTER WRITTEN IN PENCIL ON THE BACK OF AN ENVELOPE

"Thurs. Nov5, 1921/ My dear uncle Bado:—I am please to inform you I am still living at Willard State Hospital,/ Willard county, New York State. Today I am on parole again. I was outside this afternoon but/ I did not stay very long because it is very cold. /I am doing a bit of work in my ward. Uncle Bado, I am surprise what become of Uncle Rogue. I wrote to him/ but it came back to me. If you know where he is living, please tell me so I can write/ to him again. We are having our fall season now. It is getting

colder, the leaves of the trees almost gone within a month me think we shall have snow. How do you like our/ new Governor General? I hope you will write to me and please tell me what kind of government/ position you are holding now. Please send my pension early in the month [written above this line "(make it a hundred dollars if you can make it.)"] . . . my/ best regard to all Farewell!/ Your loving Nephew,/ PS—I have no definite knowledge yet when I shall obtain my freedom./ Rodrigo D. L-.

Even though he seemed to consider himself deprived of his liberty rather than hospitalized for treatment, there is no evidence that he was actively resistant, and Lagon was apparently seen as a model patient. During his decades at Willard, he was well liked by the staff because he was neat and quiet, helped around the ward, and did not cause any disturbances. It was noted over the years that he read a lot, was well versed in current events, and that he frequently wrote poetry and songs. Despite the fact that he heard voices, he was never given any psychiatric medications.

Sometime during his sixties, the voices stopped. This was noted in 1968 by a social worker who was asked to determine whether Lagon was a candidate for family care: "The 51 years of institutionalization appears to have been a mistake as far as duration, as this man appears in perfect mental condition now." Still, he remained hospitalized for another thirteen years. His health began to decline. He lost sight in one eye, and the sight in the other grew worse with time. Marie Schmidt, R.N., ran a ward for people with visual impairments at Willard in the 1970s, and she recalls Rodrigo Lagon:

MS: *He had a visual impairment, I think it was a combination of a cataract and glaucoma and he could see . . . I think he saw shadows. He used a cane to ambulate. I think he used the cane partly for his own stability and also to find objects. It wasn't a white cane, it was just a regular cane, but it aided him.*

DP: *What can you tell me about him?*

MS: *Mr. L— was a very quiet, reserved man. He was able to take care of most of his own personal needs. He would help with one particular patient who was a little Japanese man and Mr. L— always took responsibility to make sure that he—this little Japanese man— got to the bathroom and got to meals. He would always guide him to the day room. I don't think they interacted much, because I think there was a language barrier there. But he sort of took care of him.*

His blindness put an end to the staff's pressure on Rodrigo to go to a Family Care home, which he had refused to consider for more than a decade. He maintained his interest in political affairs and in reading, and the staff took him regularly to the hospital library to select Talking Books. At the age of seventy-eight, his record states that he had cancer of the bowel, which was "partially resolved 1-24-77 by surgery. Monthly Oncology Clinic to monitor possible recurrence."

When Rodrigo Lagon died in the Willard Infirmary in 1981 at the age of eighty-three, an autopsy revealed the cause of death to be "metastatic carcinoma of the liver, kidneys and lungs." No mention was made in the record of his burial. His brain was removed and sent to the neuropathology department of the New York Psychiatric Institute at Columbia University for study. One wonders what they hoped to find.

4.
IN PERMANENT LIMBO
SHE KEPT ASKING FOR DISPENSATION (UNTIL HER DOCTOR TURNED INTO THE DEVIL INCARNATE)

"A limbo large and broad, since called the Paradise of Fools, to few unknown"
—JOHN MILTON, Paradise Lost III/495

"The Hindus, Mahometans, Scandinavians, and Roman Catholics have devised a place between Paradise and "Purgatory" to get rid of a theological difficulty. If there is no sin without intention, then infants and idiots cannot commit sin, and if they die cannot be consigned to the purgatory of evil-doers; but, not being believers or good-doers, they cannot be placed with the saints. The Roman Catholics place them in the Paradise of Infants and the Paradise of Fools." —E. COBHAM BREWER, *Dictionary of Phrase and Fable*

One of the smaller, more spartan items unearthed in the attic was a tattered doctor's bag bearing several poorly legible tags. Barely held together by its frame, its fake alligator skin going to shreds, it contained a curious mixture of things: a worn-out Ace Bandage, small bottles with dried-out tincture of iodine and gold leaf; black shoelaces and a hollow red apple filled with buttons, needles, notions, and findings. A bounty of religious items commingled with the remnants of domesticity and handicraft: a small piece of white wool pinned to

some red silk with buttonhole stitches bearing the embroidered writing "Behold the heart that has loved men so much" with a heart in the center ringed in thorns with a cross on top, flames and rays emanating all around. On the bottom it says "100 Day Indulgences." There are several loose votive cards with inscriptions: "OUR LADY OF PERPETUAL HELP," "Lord thy Will be Done/Behold I am thy Handmaid," "I love Thee, I want Thee, I know that Thou art here," among many others.

And further down in the recesses of the bag, everything covered with desiccated acorn seeds, sat a well-worn Bible with dozens more votive cards and hand-scribbled notes as page holders, address books, notes, hymnals, and a package of letters, postcards, calling cards—an entire life thrown together in a space made to hold just a few doctor's tools. Ironically, many other Willard patients brought doctor's bags with them that ended up on top of the luggage pile extracted from the attic. But none of them held as potent a distillate of a life bundled together by religious devotion and a fight for soul survival.

Not surprisingly, the owner of the bag was a person of the cloth, a woman who had chosen the path of abdication and devoted herself to an earthly life of spiritual work. She was born Therese Lehner in the Bavarian village of Pöesing/Oberpfalz, which has been on record since the year 869. Her father, George, was a widower, and she seemed to have just a few cousins in nearby towns.

Unlike most other suitcase owners, Theresa's story did not come together so easily. Even though her single bag contained a great deal of information, she had changed her name, her medical record had been misfiled and appeared rather miraculously after a search of several years, and in the course of her confinement at Willard, she became one of the more disturbed people in the entire group. Therefore, a posthumous pasting-together of her life is not simply an exercise in puzzle-gamesmanship, but an act of redemption. There are many reasons to consider the writing of Theresa's story an act of "recovery," a healing afterlife, something her Dominican Sisters would wholeheartedly endorse. In fact, talking to some of the Sisters of their Order in their large convent at Sparkill, New York, overlooking the Hudson River, one can feel a deep sense of awe and puzzlement comes up at the mentioning of this story about their Sister lost to madness who never received the burial due to a Christian woman.

Thus Sister Marie Ursuline's story comes together with hesitation, pausing at every turn. We are struck by the enormity of her emotional pain, and the futility of any remedial efforts sixty years after she died. Eerily, Father Henri-Dominique Lacordaire, the biographer of St. Dominic, the founder of the order she joined, had this as his motto: "Time will hold this pen when I am gone; and to Time I leave without fear or jealousy the duty of completion." Even more surprisingly, this quote is contained in a small biography of Mother Antonina Fischer, a Dominican prioress who recruited the sixteen-year-old Theresa from Germany for the long trip across the ocean.

It is worth including a glimpse of the serpentine tale that surrounds Mother Antonina Fischer, as it provides major clues to Sister Marie's unraveling. A picture of Mother Antonina shows a towering woman, supported by a stack of books, a snarling bastion of religious fortitude in a sea of uncertainty. She must have been a very powerful anchor for the young women like Theresa who had jettisoned all worldly ties and placed their lives in the hands of her religious authority. When Mother Antonina was ousted from her post as prioress of the convent in Great Bend, Kansas, by the bishop of Chicago, for reasons too bizarre and complicated to explain here, several of the young nuns who had attached themselves to her fell prey to total confusion. Amazingly, we have a dual record of the moment when Sister Ursuline was confronted with her fate, and how she responded. A copy of the letter she sent to Bishop Hennessy turned up in the tattered doctor's bag, as well as in the Archives of the Dominican Sisters in Great Bend.

"Excuse me, your Lordship that I bother you but I have no other choice, therefore I must turn to you. On Friday, May 13 (1910), I had to go to Great Bend but I did not know why. Four years ago I made my final profession in Great Bend to Mother Antonina Fischer. On Saturday, May 14, I was called to a room next to Father Heimann, Mother Seraphine, the next prioress, Sister Bona, Sister Louise. Father Heimann read a letter written by you and gave a little talk. Within a half hour everything was over with me. After the little talk Father Heimann asked whether I would want to remain even after Mother Seraphine was prioress. I said no. . . . After that Father Heimann demanded I take off the habit and without money and clothing be sent away. And that day, May 14, I had to sign my name. I was frightened and got the idea that it would be better to run away than have the habit taken from me without cause. And I did run away as a Sister to Windhorst to pack my belongings and from there I came to Ellinwood to the Sisters because I did not want to go back to the world. Now I would like to go with Mother Antonina because I was rejected at Great Bend and do not know where to go. I would also like to know if I am free from my final vows because Father Heimann sent me away. Also I do not know if I can go to confession and Communion. I must and will trust God. Yes, the dear Lord must help me because I did not want to run away but was forced to do so.
Respectfully
Sr. M. Ursuline, O.S.D.

The paper which Sister Ursuline was expected to sign reads as follows:

I_____being of sound mind and memory and fully understanding the import of these presents, do hereby declare, in the presence of the undersigned witnesses, that of my own free will and accord I leave, never to return to the community of the Nuns of the Third Order of St. Dominic of Great Bend, Kans. and that I renounce any and all claims upon said community . . .

The apostolic delegate, Bishop Joseph Tihen, gave the following opinion of this procedure:

. . . there seems to have been an altogether irregular mode of procedure adopted, inasmuch as the person in question was allowed to leave the convent without any provision whatever having been made concerning a dispensation from her vows, which were, and are, in full force. This matter of obtaining a dispensation from the vows prescinds from the question of worthiness or unworthiness to remain in a community. It should be attended to in all cases of the dismissal of a religious from a community . . .

This situation haunted Sr. Ursuline/Theresa for the remainder of her life. She remained in a limboland from which only madness offered escape. Did she sign this document or not? Did she receive dispensation from her vows, or not? Bishop Hennessy never answered her letter.

Sister Ursuline/Theresa and three others stuck by their mother superior and traveled around the country together in search of a home. They knocked on closed doors in Baltimore, Brooklyn, Wichita, and, again, in Great Bend. On May 23, 1911, they sought acceptance to the St. Aloysius School and Convent in Colusa, California. The school's prioress had doubts whether she could accede those wishes, and once again, no permission was forthcoming from Bishop Hennessy. The little band moved on to San Jose. The Sisters at the mission there inquired whether the women were entitled to receive the sacraments or whether they should be considered as excommunicated. They moved on and then tried to gain entry into a situation in South Dakota, but nothing worked out for the small band of nuns until they found a new home in the northeast corner of North Dakota. They taught the children of hardy settlers from Austria, Germany, and Scandinavia in the remote community of Fingal, North Dakota, enduring much hardship from 1913 to 1916, when they returned to California. Sister Ursuline, however, was no longer with them. She had left North Dakota at some point for unknown reasons and made her way to New York.

The frontier of North Dakota experienced a bit of a boom in the 1910s, when many settlers moved west, coming mostly from German and northern European countries. The 133 souls of Fingal, where Sr. Ursuline taught high school for two years, today still claims 56 percent northern European ancestry. The newly built Soo Railroad connected Fairmont, where Mother

Antonina had established a tiny convent, with Fingal; quite possibly Sr. Ursuline was sent up there alone, or with one other sister at the most, to teach the children of those isolated farmers.

Mother Antonina's fortunes in this forsaken corner of the West plummeted nearly as soon as they began. Getting on in age, ailing, struggling with the unforgiving winters and still under harsh critique from the bishop of Wichita, Mother Antonina could not keep her little band together. As soon as the clouds of disapproval made their way north from Kansas over the Great Plains, the hearts of the little sisters began to shrivel once again, and their fledgling mothership crumbled away. Sr. Marie pined for her family and desperately tried to get in touch with her father in Germany. Once she was severed from the little band of sisters-in-arms, probably already by the time she was teaching in Fingal, she had to fall back on her own resources, which had never been well developed, given her early dedication to a life of the cloth. Nuns live under strict rules and leadership, but are taken care of physically and emotionally, and are firmly embedded in a structure that gives one complete purpose in life while looking after one's basic material needs. For Sr. Marie, her banishment from the motherhouse where she obtained her final vows meant an even stronger attachment to the mother superior who had been condemned by her peers and superiors for reasons beyond our comprehension.

For some reason, in the biography of Mother Antonina, Sister Marie Ursuline's last name is always misspelled and her birth date given as January 28, 1880. She entered Holy Cross Convent in Ratisbon (Regensburg), Germany, on May 29, 1896; received her habit on April 28, 1898; and made first profession on May 6, 1899. She arrived in Kansas around 1903 and made final profession on July 28, 1905. She left Great Bend on May 18, 1910, and for a while stayed with Mother Antonina in California. Her name appeared for the last time in documents of the order in the letter written by Mother Pia to the bishop.

Back in New York, Sr. Marie found refuge among the Dominican Sisters of the Sick Poor on Manhattan's Upper West Side, continued to write letters requesting dispensation, but was also prepared "to go into the world" by ordering music and improving her organ-playing skills, possibly wanting to become a church organist or piano teacher. In the spring of 1918, with the war over, she once again tried to get in touch with her father, but the letter was never sent. She became portlier and needed a new habit for the summer. She received a letter from Sister Yolanda in Brooklyn, a close friend, who discouraged her from trying to teach the piano: "believe me, you don't know enough to give lessons. You can give embroidery lessons . . . but above all make yourself useful, help around, and try and get a little thinner . . . take my advice and rise early in the morning. Don't give scandal to the other sisters who work so hard and are up so early every morning . . ." (April 16, 1918).

Her despair mounted, as evidenced by a letter written on April 21, 1918, to Mother Peter, prioress at the Brooklyn convent: "I'm not feeling very well, suffer a great deal with headache. Over two years I have not heard from my dear father. This is very sad indeed. . . . The time will never come for me to see my dear father again. For I have made up my mind, never to cross the ocean, and this for many reasons. Some time ago, I have asked for my dispensation. Please pray for me Venerable Mother Peter. You see that I need prayers very bad. Wishing you heavenly peace which the world cannot give . . ."

The last letter she drafted was addressed to The Most Reverend John Bonzano, the Apostolic Delegate in Washington, D.C., and predated her admission to Bellevue Hospital by a mere three weeks.

> *I, Sister Mary Ursuline L.—, O.S.D. is asking Your Excellency for my dispensation as soon as possible. I, Sister Mary Ursuline L.—, have made my final vows at Great Bend, Kansas, in the hands of the Right Reverend John Joseph Hennessy D.D. Bishop of Wichita, Kansas. I'm the Sister that was to see Your Excellency about three years ago. . . . Our Community in North Dakota is dispended [sic], and so I don't belong to any community. And as no other community will take me in because I'm not in good health. I remember that Your Excellency had asked me if I wanted dispensation. And I have refused to take dispensation because I had hoped to get back to one of my own communities that is either back to Brooklyn or to Kansas. But it is in vain—I'm refused by both.*

Two weeks later, on June 27, 1918, she stood before Judge Pendleton, who certified her for commitment to a state hospital based on the findings of Doctors Theron, Vosburgh, and Brink of Bellevue Hospital. Sr. Ursuline had probably been there no more than a week. Their report to the judge described her as "excited, noisy and destructive . . . her general manner is silly and childish, she is very impulsive and becomes so restless that she has to be restrained. She runs about in a nude condition, is playful and shows psychomotor overactivity. Is evidently a mentally defective. Her replies to questions are irrelevant, evasive, as she says 'I don't know.' No extent information can be obtained from her."

How a person could be transformed almost overnight from a writer of coherent letters to a "childish . . . and mentally defective" person is hard to fathom. On the other hand, what choice did she have? To keep wearing a habit that might have been sinful for her to wear? To keep impersonating the nun she was no longer allowed to be? Wear the scapular and veil one day, and trade them in for a business suit the next? Were there any signs in the buildup to that day in June 1918 when she stood before the judge, seemingly feebleminded and incoherent? She certainly was despondent and desperate about her religious (and worldly) status, which were both in suspense. But she kept herself active nevertheless, kept knocking on doors, even though her knocks became progressively muter, muffled by the sadness that had engulfed her, no longer feeling that she could succeed in her umpteenth attempt to have her situation resolved by some ecclesiastical authority. But the day of relinquishing her fighting stance came sooner than expected. Nearly from one day to the next, she dropped her resolve and her Ferris Waist, exchanging her grown-up personality for the kind of regressed demeanor that we expect from young children throwing a tantrum, but not from a well-educated schoolteacher who stood her ground in the prairie of North Dakota.

What does "regression" mean in the context of psychosis, schizophrenia, or dementia praecox, as Sr. Marie was diagnosed in 1918? This term comes from a model of mental functioning that talks about layers of consciousness and more or less developed levels of mental activity; each one peeled off gives way to another, "lower" level, the childish, more "primitive" aspects of the personality. The model used by biological psychiatry to explain so-called schizophrenia or dementia praecox is generally the opposite: it posits a brain-based process that injects toxins into itself, a coursing of excessive humors, a sprouting of malignant neurons, almost cancerlike, that overrides anything sensible, focused, or adult. To understand what might have happened to Sr. Ursuline, we need to resort to a more dynamic model, one that permits the assumption that under certain circumstances, the mind finds a radical solution by relinquishing its attachment to conventional reality and gives way to the very opposites of the principles the person had followed all her life. A nun running naked is an almost comical but highly relevant example of such an unleashing. Sinfulness takes over but can only do so in the guise of madness. Feeblemindedness is not feigned, it simply permits the person to abandon all responsibility, obviously at the risk of falling prey to the workings of the psychiatric system.

If she had lived at another time or in another place, Theresa might have been subjected to some kind of exorcism or another church-sanctioned ritual to drive the madness/devil out of her. And under certain circumstances, such an unconventional approach might even have succeeded, especially if the person understood that the church was taking charge once again, bringing her back into the fold, albeit in a rather brutal manner. On the other hand, and not unlike the fate of many predecessors who went mad without being sanctified, she might have suffered torture and even death at the stake.

For Theresa, entering the mental health system meant relinquishing all traces of her former life. On her admission sheet to Willard the word *unknown* was entered eleven times, encompassing her date of birth, her parents' names, her education, and even her religion. This was more than a year after she was brought to Bellevue Hospital in Manhattan, during which time the staff would have had ample opportunity to investigate her background further.

No one knew or believed that she was wearing a habit until a few days before admission, and that for all practical purposes, she was still considered a fully professed member of a religious order and had never received dispensation. It was not for lack of information that the hospital never acknowledged her religious background and the centrality of her spiritual conflict. At her admission interview to Manhattan State Hospital on June 28, 1918, Theresa said: "I don't hear voices, I don't see visions. I feel silly—I am not crazy—I am nervous. I had an operation for gall-stones three and one half or four and one half years ago in North Dakota. I am in New York four years only. I live at 140 West 61st Street with the Sisters of the Sick Poor. I was stubborn. I did not want to steal. They said I had a pull. I got excited over the war. I am all mixed up. I feel down hearted."

She herself was trying to draw a line between her condition and certifiable madness: "silly" versus "crazy," "nervous" but not hearing voices. Did she attribute her nervousness to the operation in North Dakota? She reveals something that never gets explained anywhere: "I was stubborn. I did not want to steal. They said I had a pull." A major infraction, something she did against her better knowledge, under the influence of an external power, a malicious force, maybe the devil. But no one believed what she explicitly told them. The doctors ignored her spiritual woes and apparently chose to assume that her entire existence prior to coming to the hospital was a figment of her imagination. They treated her like a mad, newborn child, and she acted accordingly.

On February 19, 1919, Marie was among a group of 116 men and women put on a train up the Hudson River from Manhattan State Hospital under an order of transfer by the New York State Hospital Commission. When spoken to, Marie "put her head down on the table and said: I want to get out of here, I'm just pulled around and treated like a fool all my life." She had "been pulled" away from her parental home into a convent, shipped across the ocean, traveled thousands of miles zigzagging around America, fled back to New York City, and was now in a mess of mad folks sent up the river. No wonder she also had a "pull" in another direction.

At Willard, she started to work in the sewing room. Two months after her arrival she began to resist, was "stubborn . . . and gave trouble in the tailor shop. Exposed herself to men [*sic*] patients and refused to work." As a result, she was thereafter kept on the ward. Sexuality is as frowned upon in state hospitals as it is in religious convents. Women and men are kept in separate quarters, masturbation will land you in hell, public display of sexuality will get you a trip to the madhouse. Being treated like a fool, you soon start acting like one.

Inserted between pages 372 and 373 of her prayer book:

Prayer to St. Jude Thaddeus. Apostle and Martyr.
To be said in great affliction, or when one seems to be deprived of all visible help, and for cases despaired of.

Saint Jude, glorious Apostle, faithful servant and friend of Jesus...Pray for me, who am so miserable; make use, I implore you, of that particular privilege accorded to you, to bring visible and speedy help where help was almost despaired of. Come to my assistance in this my great need that I may receive the consolations and succor of heaven in all my necessities, tribulations and sufferings . . .

Time flies at Willard, at least when measured by the frequency of observations entered in a patient's record. In Marie's case this happened about every three months. "At times is assaultive," "usually remains alone," "smiles and responds when spoken to," "has a sexual trend." In December 1920, things seemed to take an even more bizarre turn. She began to claim that "there were live chickens inside her hatched from eggs she had eaten." Becoming more suspicious, especially about the food given to her, she took to scraping her bread carefully before eating it. And on March 24, 1922, she had a physical altercation with two female attendants, "pounding (one) severely" and nearly tearing the uniform off the other one, which landed her on a more "secure" ward in Chapin Hall. We can't know what prompted this altercation, which was described as an "assault" on the staff member. Such attacks are rarely unprovoked. No paranoia was noted when Marie was brought to Bellevue Hospital three years earlier, and neither at Manhattan State Hospital, nor for the first two years at Willard. Either she turned against the institution or the institution turned against her. It was a match made in Hell.

Inserted between pages 108 and 109 of her prayer book:

Prayer

Look down upon me, good and gentle Jesus, while before Thy face I humbly kneel, and burning soul pray and beseech thee, to fix deep in my heart lively sentiments of faith, hope and charity, true contrition for my sins, and a firm purpose of amendment; the while I contemplate with great love and tender pity, Thy five wounds, pondering over them within me, while I recall to mind the words with David, Thy prophet, said of Thee, my Jesus: "They pierced my hands and my feet. They numbered all my bones."

Things soon quieted down for Marie at Chapin Hall and she was sent back to a more easygoing ward after a few months. State hospitals today still have these kind of "secure" or "special treatment units" where patients are placed when they are deemed too unruly or dangerous on other wards. Treatment there consists of aggressive pharmacology and behavioral control. In those years at Willard, drugs were used only rarely, mainly barbiturates or chloral hydrate if someone was completely out of control. Given their serious risks, including death, if used excessively or not monitored properly, doctors avoided using these drugs whenever possible. Instead, they liberally used restrictions and physical restraint. Apparently, Marie became calmer without medication, another sign that her "paranoia" was related to her environment; a change in personnel and the way they approached her had dramatic effect.

Inserted between pages 104 and 105 of Theresa's prayer book:

A Wish

I wish I could really and truly
Could pray with an earnest mind
To be humbled, despised, forgotten,
In the Cross true joy to find.

Oh! I wish I could wish for suffering,
May it be my only pride
To be trodden even as the dust,
To know but my God crucified.

For heaven is won by much suffering,
No cross, then no crown to gain;
Ah me! It is hard to be holy if we
Shrink from every pain.

If a trifling word of unkindness
Maketh the heart sick and faint,
My good God, oh change me,
Or never shall I be a saint.

In the next couple of years, Marie (who now called herself "Tressa") was transferred back and forth several times, was said to harbor many "absurd" delusions, and became assaultive at times. Clearly she had become mired in a rather demoralizing cycle. And yet, once again, she started to write letters.

Respectful Mr. Biswick [did she have access to a typewriter, or did someone take the time to transcribe this letter, dated June 22, 1925?]

Dear Sir,
By addressing you as respectful, I mean that I really do not know you from no place. And that of course means, you my dear sir are very unknown to me Miss Tressa L.— The principal thing of a fact *off* [sic] *which I have heard, first by cold wirering* [sic] *then by warm wirering* [sic] *which were the very true words of Miss Wright Nurse of Ward 2.*
Therefor dear sir Biswick let me know the truth, if this is really your desire to adopt me as your darling child, then to be engaged for nine months and then to marry me *as your lawful wife?*
So if this is all true and I will really and truly give my full consent. *Since I was put in Erkul and disgust, I am trying very hard to find out my real real parents. But up to now I did not succeed, which is very shameful indeed.*
Dear sir Biswick I was never engaged nor ever married. I have but only one child which should be a boy and one dog a Daxel of which both I should be the real mother—must close my letter. Present I'm in Ward 9. I will give this letter into the hands of head nurse Miss Hilliard, Ward 1.
Yours truly
Respecful Tressa L.—
Ward 9

Pretty crazy stuff—or not. The mother of a dachshund, parthenogenetically conceived? Cold and warm wiring? Overheard conversations of nurses and attendants? Who is this Mr. Biswick and where is Erkul? Theresa acted like a parentless child, ready to be adopted and married off at the same time. Left to her own devices, without any type of dialogue or therapy, a person in such a "regressed" and vulnerable state of mind is likely to conjure up all kinds of confused and confusing scenarios. It is unlikely that Theresa ever had any type of sex education, but she probably knew how children were conceived and that humans don't give birth to dachshunds. But maybe she did feel like a mother to a dog she grew up with, in her long-ago Bavarian home, where her mother died and left her to an uncertain fate at an early age.

Over the next few years, she continued to write letters to unknown men seeking to be married. She still carried chickens inside and wanted them taken out. "When crossed in any way she will scold and sometimes assault patients." In one of those letters she writes to a "Professor Chanar," having heard that he might want to marry her, which she would be perfectly happy to do, she promises to be a good wife and begs him to transfer her at once. As confused as this letter may be, it is a mixture of factual and imagined information. Professor Chanar was also known as Dr. Morrison, who gave birth to "Mina Cleevan" (Theresa's alleged real name), on January 29, 1912, in Great Bend, Kansas (when she was actually thirty two years old, and may have had her gallbladder surgery). Then she tells parts of her true life story: "I was a Dominican Nun for some years. I entered the Dominican Sisters of Brooklyn, New York. The Parish Church is Trinity Church Rev. Father Dauffenbach was the Pastor and Mother Antonina Fischer was the Prioress when I entered."

To read this letter onlyly as evidence of a deranged mind means forgoing an opportunity to connect with its author, who was obviously confused by messages she was getting through the walls of the institution and the veritable memories of her life. To help her sort these out might not have been an easy task, but no one ever thought of attempting it.

From page 86 of her prayer book:

My dear Lord, you most beloved wealth, who can never be sufficiently praised, loved and adored, as my heart desires to do at every moment: I want to enter into a contract of love with you, my dear Jesus: as often as my heart shall beat, as many times I shall love you completely and adore you in the holiest of sacraments of the altar.

Years went by, punctured by periods of excitement, "irritable moods," especially around those times of the month. She kept mostly to herself except when irked and bothered by fellow patients or staff, sometimes finding fault with the food, but to no avail. She worked only under duress. She was mostly neat, sometimes shouting, cursing, and feeling persecuted by staff, often muttering to herself in an undertone.

October 19, 1931:
. . . heard voices stating one of the ward nurses was going to go after
her and kill her. She ran away and broke several windows cutting her-
self about her fingers and wrists.

Were these simply the deluded vagaries of a "praecox type," or evidence of real terror in the face of abusive staff? There is no way to know for sure, but the fluctuations in Theresa's behavior must have been tied to something other than just the inner whims of a deranged mind. Staff in mental hospitals have been overheard many times making idle and not so idle threats toward their charges. Patients have died in restraints visible to all who share their quarters.

Consistently, over several years, Theresa considered herself but a child, born in 1912: sixteen, nine, ten years old, and not aging—if anything, getting younger all the time. A child grows up quickly to become a nun, a teacher of children, never marries, never has sex, is turned into a fool, a mental patient, shipped back and forth from ward to ward, homeless, parentless, waiting to be reborn, adopted, married, and have children of her own.

But age began to show itself by attacking the body. Chickens in her belly turn into swollen legs. Her delusions heat up, she is surrounded by "Kaisers, ancient Kings," and the president was "Franklin Lincoln" in 1933. Her body heats up, too, her stomach explodes in pain, she vomits, aches all over, her legs are inflamed, but she recovers. Condition: unknown; treatment: hexamethylene.

Page 78 of her prayer book:

All inner and outer suffering and indispositions, as well as all joys and com-
forts, which will come upon me today, I sacrifice to you in compassion with
the bitter suffering and death of my dear Jesus.

And her mood changes to euphoria, she is excited, expecting to be sent somewhere any day now, eleven years old and ready for a change. Makes "numerous little dolls and figures out of stockings, old blankets, etc."

In 1933, a Dr. Evans came on duty, and had considerably more to say about Theresa than any of his predecessors during the previous fourteen years. Under the heading "VOLUBLE, FRIENDLY, BIZARRE DELUSIONS OF GRANDEUR, OF A RELIGIOUS NATURE, DISORIENTED, HALLUCINATED, AUDITORY AND VISUAL," Dr. Evans dismisses her claim to be a "member of the St. Benedictine order of nuns," which he finds equally delusional as her notions of being eleven and of an imminent transfer to another ward. As far as we know, Theresa never had the opportunity to discuss religious matters with a cleric after her arrival at Willard. Her spiritual preoccupations were simply categorized as delusional ideas. No one bothered to check out whether she was indeed a nun. All they needed to do was to go through her doctor's bag stowed neatly in the attic on the women's side under the letter *L*. Her reverence for Bishop McDonald of Brooklyn did not make anyone wonder how she would have known of this person. Her thirty-eight years prior to becoming a mental patient were wiped from the historical record; no wonder she considered herself merely a babe.

From page 15 of Theresa's prayer book:

Dear Father I appeal to you through Jesus, your son, please bestow upon me the fullness of your mercy; praise the house which I inhabit, let HEIL (salvation) and TUGEND (virtue) live therein and give me strength and GNADE (mercy) so I can follow the example of Maria and always act EIL-FERTIG (promptly) and willingly on behalf of your honor and the benefit of my fellow human beings. Amen

Dr. Evans's charge over Theresa lasted for nearly five years. He seems to have known her quite well, and she sometimes considered him her "second father." Unlike many long-term patients who appear to "burn out," she continued to preoccupy herself with religious themes pertaining to life and death, her role on earth, important ancestors, and the coming redemption. In her past lives, she believed, she had been murdered many times but kept coming back in a new body. Joyously, Theresa expected to die for the final time in the near future, this being the last body she was supposed to have. In spite of these very fluid and extravagant preoccupations, Dr. Evans considered her memory for "events previous to her commitment" as quite accurate, and yet he hardly noted what she told him about that other life of hers.

Her next doctor heard a new story about her religious mission: she was the "Lordin" (maybe a German ending as in: the Lord, *Herr*, the female Lord, *Herrin*), the right hand of the Lord. He observed about Theresa: "The Lord created 'stamm-fathers' and that was the end of Paradise. She has the color for many sensations, for instance, that electricity is crimson red. She says she is 20 years old and she is double rich . . . she can hear God's voice . . . and this is a 'diamond country' and she has to have a certain weight before she can die."

The account of Theresa's last decade at Willard is hard to stomach. The chart entries get progressively grimmer, bearing witness to a great deal of physical suffering on top of her delusional preoccupations. The fact that she lived as long as she did with all the ailments she had is remarkable, but not likely due to exemplary medical care. She was a lost soul living out her years in mental and physical agony, only offset by her conviction that she would be saved one day, and by her many attempts to stay useful to the nurses on the ward. In her ailing condition, she still wanted to help out on the ward, even when told she had to stay in bed.

On December 1, 1949, at the age of sixty-nine, Sr. Marie Ursuline, O.S.D., née Theresa Lehner, was finally absolved from her earthly suffering. The record does not tell us if she received the final sacraments. Her remains were removed for dissection to the Syracuse University Medical School. The State of New York saw fit to turn her over to science and thereby deprived her of the funeral rites due to a Catholic sister. Officially, she had never received dispensation, and should have been buried in her full habit, in spite of the years she spent in the Limbo of Fools.

As a frontispiece of her prayer book, which accompanied her from Germany, all through the United States, and finally up to Willard, she affixed the following prayer:

Open up your holy heart, Dear Jesus, show me its loveliness and unite me with it for ever and ever. May every breath and every beat of my heart, even in my sleep, be a witness of my love for you, and tell you perpetually: Yes, Lord, I love you! Please kindly accept the little good that I have accomplished and bestow upon me the mercy to help me rectify the evil deeds that I committed, so that I can praise you today and forever. Amen.

5.
CHILDREN DIED
AND SHE KNIT
HER LIFE AWAY

One summer day in 1930, Mrs. Ethel Smalls felt tired and took to her bed. She was forty years old. After twenty-two years of marriage, she had just divorced her abusive husband, who drank to excess, was an unpredictable provider, and ran around with other women. As a young wife, she had two children in quick succession, then a miscarriage, and then surgery to remove an ovarian tumor. Later, she endured the death of two infant daughters: Doris, who died just a month before her first birthday; and Irma, who survived barely four weeks. Her father died of cancer shortly thereafter. That same summer of 1930, her two living children, Ruth and Harold, were both recently married, and after their parents' divorce, the

family home in Ithaca was broken up—belongings were sold, parceled out to relatives, or put into storage.

It was the Depression, and money was scarce, so Mrs. Smalls took a room in the nearby village of Freeville, bartering some furniture and her dressmaking skills for rent and board. After just a few weeks, she and the landlady had a falling out, and Ethel was ordered to leave. Instead, she said she was ill and took to bed. Two days later, the landlady called the authorities, stating that she heard Mrs. Smalls laughing in the middle of the night and that Ethel

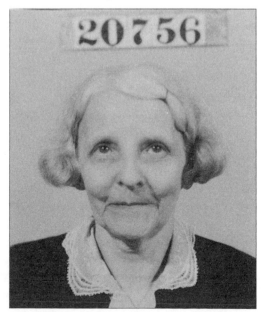

"constantly consulted the spirits about where she should go and what she should do." She was examined by her family doctor, Dr. Homer Gemung, who found her in the following condition: "Staying in bed, tongue very coated, temperature 99.1, heart rapid, seems run down and subnormal physically." The doctor noted that Ethel "exhibited no absolute delusions in our presence. She made statements that according to the best history obtainable were not true. She is in a home and refused to leave after being ordered out and used vulgar and obscene language." These observations were sufficient cause for a judge to commit her to Willard State Hospital, to which she was escorted by a nurse, a state trooper, and her doctor.

During her admission interview, Ethel Smalls was quite talkative. The examining physician viewed this as a sign of mania, although she said nothing illogical or particularly hyperbolic in the transcribed conversation. She denied the accusations made by the landlady, explaining that the two had quarreled over money and had taunted each other with hurtful gossip; she viewed the landlady's call to the authorities as simple revenge. When asked if she heard voices, Ethel did not understand the reference, and when the doctor explained what he meant, she seemed to find it both amusing and unbelievable that some people heard nonexistent voices. She freely described numerous physical ailments, and believed that Dr. Gemung suggested that she needed a rest. Since neither her elderly mother nor her newly married daughter were able to care for her, Ethel Smalls agreed to stay at Willard for a rest cure.

SPIRITS ABOUND

The village of Freeville, both then and now, was home to the Spiritualist Center of America, a retreat founded in 1897 where spiritualists from across the English-speaking world gather to hear preachers, consult with healers, and cultivate contact with the spirits that they believe survive death. Modern Spiritualism, as opposed to the belief in a spirit world common among the animist religions of indigenous peoples, arose in the mid-nineteenth century during a wave of Christian religious fervor in western and central New York. Around the same time and in the same area, Joseph Smith founded Mormonism, and a farmer named William Miller predicted that the Second Coming would occur in 1844, sparking the Millerist sect. The apparent failure of his prediction did not stop his following from growing exponentially, eventually becoming known as the Seventh-Day Adventists. A number of Shaker communities and the secular utopian community of Oneida were also established in the region. The Shaker and Oneida communities vanished by the end of the nineteenth century. But the Spiritualists in Freeville continued to thrive, building a meetinghouse, visitors' cottages, a hotel, and a dining hall to accommodate the many seekers who arrived on the Lehigh Valley or New York Central Railroads, which converged there. Spiritualism was especially popular during and just after World War I, as grieving families of dead soldiers sought evidence that their sons', brothers', and husbands' spirits were still lingering around.

The Spiritualist compound, a large collection of whitewashed clapboard structures, was the center of activity in Freeville during this time, and much of the small town's economy was based on feeding, housing, and transporting the visitors. The energy emanating from this place in 1930, when thousands of seekers from all over the country came to commune with the spirits, would have been hard to ignore for anyone living nearby, especially someone like Ethel, who had lost two children and had been beaten by her husband.

Ethel Smalls was a devout woman, active in church work and service to the poor. But if she came to Freeville as a spiritual seeker, perhaps wishing to contact her dead children, there is nothing in her medical record or among her papers that speaks to this issue. While Ethel, perhaps strategically, denied during her admission interview that she consulted the spirits, such behavior would not have seemed at all unusual in the village of Freeville during the time she lived there.

THE PARSON'S DAUGHTER

Born in 1889 in Ithaca, Ethel Black Smalls was one of three children of a minister and his wife. What little is known about her childhood, which was apparently unremarkable, came from her admission interview and discussions the staff had with her brother and sister. As a youngster she was especially interested in music, playing the piano and singing in the church choir; as an adult, she continued these avocations and headed the music committee at her church. Ethel completed the eleventh grade, and in 1908 married Seymour Smalls. "I was eighteen and foolish," she remarked to a doctor at Willard who asked about her marital history. She described difficult births, a miscarriage, and her husband's lack of help when she faced a sudden need for surgery:

"You see that there was three children right along and I was weak. Then the doctor said the trouble was 'You have got an ovarian tumor and you will have to have it removed.' I was frightened of a hospital, and only 22 years old. My father was a Methodist minister and came and got me and took me to the hospital and left the children with my mother." She also complained about the abuse of a frequently drunken husband, and said that he took little interest in the children. "I had to be mother and father both with my children."

Mrs. Smalls was a seamstress of exceptional skill, and during the 1910s and 1920s, she supported herself and her children by taking in sewing, as her husband, a plumber by trade, had difficulty keeping a job. The bags she packed for her one-way journey to Willard contained no clothing, souvenirs, or practical personal items, only her silver flatware, a Bible with three family photos tucked between the pages, and beautiful evidence of her handiwork.

> 20756.2 *Quilt cover, hand-sewn appliqué cotton quilt top made up of 6 by 7 approximately 10" squares of crossed tulip patterns (three buds, one facing each corner, leaves and ground in 4th corner). White ground green with red in center of bud. Border of individual appliqué leaves in faded green or blue fabric. Nicely constructed. Outside edge has a machine stitched narrow rolled hem. Condition: good. Faded and stained fabric is sound.*

> 20756.4 *Quilt. Variation on the nine patch. Nicely made. Red and pink small floral pattern cotton with white, 5 squares by 5 squares with a band between each square. Border of pink white pink strips with small reverse nine patch in each corner. Quilt stitched by hand in an X-pattern on each square of the nine patch and straight line on bands in between. Ethel written in ink on back corner. Back white cotton, probably cotton filling. Condition: Good, some staining and dirt.*

> 20756.38 *White linen square table cover, triangular shaped fillet lace crochet in each corner, overcast crochet edging on rest. In flat areas between corners embroidered flower design, white on white. Condition: stained. Matching design to 20756.39*

But the loveliest pieces of needlework found in Ethel's suitcase are much more personal: a christening gown with exquisitely detailed embroidery, finely worked matching baby booties, and other garments probably made for the infants who died.

> 20756.26 *Baby's dress, white cotton dimity with delicate crochet front panel side inserts and border around hem. Three pearl button back closure. Four narrow vertical tucks at center front. Machine and hand sewn. Condition: good, some staining and yellowing.*

> 20756.27 *Baby cotton flannel nightgown, white with blue silk embroidered feather stitch at neck. One pearl button and narrow blue ribbon draw string and tie at center back neck. Blue silk blanket stitch decorative edging at sleeve edge and feather stitch with ribbon threaded through at edge creating a narrow ruffle. Machine sewn, hand finished. Condition: good, minor staining.*

> 20756.31 *Baby knitted cap, cream base with pink band at neck and face. Pink ribbon laced through neck and ties in front rosette at each side. Condition: good.*

> 20756.32a, b *White linen baby booties with white embroidery on toe. Hand sewn. Condition: some staining and yellowing.*

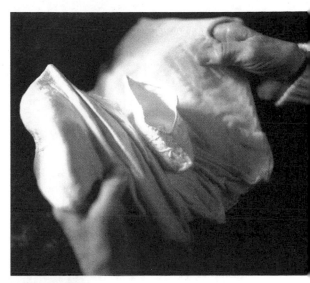

A HOST OF PHYSICAL COMPLAINTS

Ethel Smalls entered Willard with a number of physical complaints, and these only got worse over the years. Ethel believed that she was in the hospital to cure her medical problems, and she never asked to be released, as these problems continued to plague her for as long as she lived. Her symptoms of back pain, headaches, gastrointestinal upsets, and severe menstrual periods were dismissed as hypochondria or malingering by the Willard doctors. Today, Mrs. Smalls might be diagnosed with somatization disorder, a diagnosis describing mental and emotional distress expressed as physical symptoms, although with a history of abdominal surgery for ovarian tumors, she certainly had a physical substrate that gave rise to these endless complaints. Ethel clearly preferred to think of herself as suffering from physical ailments rather than accepting her various psychiatric diagnoses, like manic depression and schizophrenia, for which there is scant evidence in the record. The reports of her mental condition belabored her over-talkativeness (which she readily acknowledged), and her habit of dissembling, primarily by exaggerating her family's wealth and social status. These were annoying traits, no doubt, but hardly evidence of psychosis.

Yet as a physically abused woman who had dealt with a miscarriage and the death of two babies, she certainly had cause for a great deal of emotional pain. No emotional outbursts or signs of depression showed up in her record ("That's not my nature," Ethel responded when specifically questioned by a doctor). Rather, she was almost resolutely cheerful, except when it came to discussing her physical symptoms, and often industrious, helping around the ward in a rather officious manner, and tending to her perennial needlework. Maybe her emotional pain instead became manifest in her frequent complaints of vague pain, nausea, and worry about her heart and gallbladder.

AUGUST 23, 1933: *This patient is in fair physical health. She eats and sleeps well and is a good ward worker. She is quiet, agreeable and causes no particular trouble on the ward, but is always talking about herself and her ailments. She expresses no other delusions or hallucinations.* —Dr. Strong

JANUARY 12, 1948: *Patient has remained in good physical health since last noted although she is constantly complaining of many ailments. She does assist a little with ward work but thinks she is doing a wonderful lot of work and the employees would be unable to get along without her. Sometimes she is very bossy. She takes some interest in her environment and converses with others. She is clean in habits and keeps her clothes tidy.*
—Dr. E. R. Laughlin

The doctors' initial belief that she was hypochondriacal led them to ignore certain symptoms of real injury and disease. Mrs. Smalls broke her wrist in a fall early in her stay, but it was never set, and she complained of pain and had limited range of motion thereafter. She also told anyone who would listen that she had a spinal injury at birth that caused constant backaches. Staff dismissed this as malingering, and not until she was X-rayed after a fall did the doctors find the evidence of her scoliosis.

> JUNE 25, 1962: *Patient is a 72 year old female who resides in Ward 8 Pines. She is agreeable, cooperative, tidy, neat, and well oriented in all spheres. She denies hallucinations, and homicidal or suicidal ideation not elicited. Patient thinks she had a spine injury at birth. Her left arm has been in a sling for about two months—infection (old left radial fracture, about 30 years ago). Patient is occasionally visited by relatives, but says she cannot go home as yet because she thinks she is not yet strong enough.*
>
> —*L. Kerschbaumer, M.D.*

LIFE (AND DEATH) ON THE WARD

Ethel Smalls showed a sadly facile ability to adapt herself to institutional life. Just a week after her arrival, Dr. Rexford noted that "Patient since admission has gotten along very comfortably, has been compliant, agreeable, assisting about the ward, has been moderately social with patients and nurses. When greeted she responds promptly." A month later, she was "friendly and good natured, and generally in a happy mood and lively." According to the doctor, she denied all the statements made in the commitment papers. But oddly enough, he also mentioned that it was "difficult to get her to express any abnormal ideas."

Ethel also responded to ward life in a way that might not be expected of a woman with her religious background:

> AUGUST 20, 1930: *It was discovered yesterday that she and Miss G., another patient, had been in the habit of getting into bed together, probably at night, but they were found in bed together in the day time and said to be having a jolly time. When discovered by Miss McMahon, charge attendant of the ward, they giggled and chuckled and told her there was a place for her if she would like to get in.*   —*Dr. Rexford*

It is surprising to find such a straightforward and seemingly non-judgmental statement about lesbian sexuality in a psychiatric record from 1930, but in fact there were consequences involved. Ethel was immediately transferred to another ward, and it is doubtful that she and Miss G. had the opportunity to spend any more time alone together.

For the next forty-three years, the notes in her record tell a fairly consistent story of Ethel Small's restricted life as a patient. Except for her frequent physical complaints, she was "compliant, well-behaved, industrious, and pleasant" to most people she encountered. She did not shirk from helping around the ward, but also had a bossy streak, expecting others to do things her way. She bragged about her family's non-existent wealth, and sometimes mentioned that she was engaged to a man of means. Aside from knitting and crocheting, she was also an avid reader. In later years, she watched television daily. Ethel rarely made use of her parole card to get off the ward for entertainment or outdoor activities. Her grown children apparently visited her only once, early on, but her brother and sister came to see her several times a year, sometimes taking her out for a car ride. She was never given any psychiatric medications, and by her sixties, no psychiatric symptoms at all were noted in the record. As she grew older, doctors and social workers approached her with the notion of moving to a nursing home or to a foster family for adults, but Ethel refused, pointing to her medical problems. After a bout of pneumonia in 1972, she developed congestive heart failure, and her condition gradually worsened, until she died in her sleep a year later at the age of 83. Unlike most of her fellow patients, Ethel Smalls had relatives who kept in touch with her during her entire stay, and her brother Ellis Black had her buried in the family plot in Trumansburg, New York.

WOMEN, TRAUMA, AND PSYCHIATRY

Throughout history, violence and loss have sometimes driven women mad. Not that men did not suffer a similar fate at times, but women have been decidedly more often on the receiving end. Psychiatry has generally been complicit in this process. The vast majority of women, and more than half of men, in psychiatric institutions today have experienced sexual or physical abuse before and after they were diagnosed as mentally ill. Many authors who have themselves experienced trauma and psychiatric treatment have pointed out that psychiatric care often means being traumatized again; that hospital practices such as seclusion, restraint, and forced medication, whether witnessed or experienced on one's own body, are traumatic in and of themselves, and liable to worsen any pre-existing trauma-related condition, or to set off post-traumatic stress disorder for the very first time. Who can argue that a woman who is manhandled by several attendants, stripped, tied down, and forcibly injected should not experience this as a form of rape, rather than as a method of treatment? For trauma survivors, even less obviously intrusive practices, such as the regimentation of ward life, constraints on visits and communication, or the inability to take a quiet walk on the grounds, may aggravate their condition by taking away the sense of control over one's daily life that is a prerequisite for feeling safe.

Today, a woman like Ethel Smalls who enters the system at least has a chance that she might be asked "What happened to you?" rather than "What's wrong with you?" In certain places, she might even be referred to a specialist who has experience working with trauma survivors. But in the 1930s, a woman beaten by her husband and mourning her children would not have been considered a trauma survivor. In those days, only men returning from battle merited such designation, and so Ethel had to resign herself to a quiet, rudimentary life behind walls.

6.
LIKE A FLY IN
A SPIDER WEB

DR. GOLD:	*How are you?*
MD:	*Kind of tired. I have a pain on my right side.*
DR. GOLD:	*Where are you now?*
MD:	*Willard State Hospital.*
DR. GOLD:	*Why are you here?*
MD:	*I don't know.*
DR. GOLD:	*What kind of illness do we treat here?*
MD:	*Mental illness.*
DR. GOLD:	*Are you mentally ill?*
MD:	*I don't know yet.* (smiles)

—from Initial Mental Status Exam, July 3, 1941

On a June day in 1941, Margaret Dunleavy, a forty-eight-year-old tuberculousis nurse, was packed up and driven the forty miles from her job at Biggs Memorial Hospital in Ithaca, New York, to Willard State Hospital, guarded by a transfer agent and an attendant.

She had never seen a psychiatrist before. The admission papers offered the following as evidence of Margaret's need for involuntary hospitalization: "Annoys people. Accuses people of persecuting her and talking about her. Says that she has heard one of the doctors discussing her case. Says switchboard operator listens in on her conversations and that people on other floors can be heard talking about her."

As she was led away to the ward, Miss Dunleavy said that she felt "like a fly in a spider web." She had lost her job and the lodging that came with it, so she reluctantly agreed to stay at Willard until a place could be found for her to live. That never happened. Instead, she lived for decades on a psychiatric ward, dying at Willard thirty-two years later, at the age of eighty-one. Her 1939 Dodge Coupe was repossessed because she failed to make the monthly payments, and she had no access to the eighteen trunks, suitcases, boxes, and bundles of her belongings that were stored in the attic shortly after her admission.

25682.86 Box, cardboard—black with silver squares of graded sizes on the bottom and white with silver squares of graded sizes on the top, contains patterns and sewing notions: various colors of DMC cotton perle embroidery floss in unused and used skeins, packages of needles; 8 buttons, small number of safety pins, straight pins, tacks, and paperclips; 1 necklace closure, short ivory crochet hook, one button hook, lace edging, spools of cotton and silk thread, snaps and hooks and eyes, scraps of fabric, two small bars of Ivory soap, 8 paper patterns for dresses from the late 1920's early 1930's

Margaret Dunleavy's trunk had, by far, the largest accumulation of personal possessions among the suitcase owners: dishes, pots and pans, kitchen ware, small appliances, lamps, clothing, sewing notions, fabric and patterns, needlework pieces in progress, books, a few odds and ends of furniture, nurse's uniforms, framed prints and family photos, legal documents, dozens of cards and letters, and hundreds of negatives and photographs. Her belongings suggest that she was an industrious, neat, and meticulous woman whose possessions were well cared for and carefully chosen for their quality and aesthetic value.

The 1930s-era housewares, which today are sought-after collector's items, are in mint condition. Her boxes contained a Pyrex glass pitcher; an aluminum coffee percolator with a pale-green Depression Glass insert; a set of matching ridged canisters of the same green glass; enamelware pots, bowls, and basins; an Art Deco syrup pitcher; and a flatware set with colorful plastic handles. She had a taste for fine pottery: a small Japanese porcelain vase, a larger, brightly painted Italian vase; beautifully decorated blue lusterware bowls; and one delicate hand-painted bone china teacup and saucer. She also owned a small desk fan, an electric hotplate, a Baby Ben alarm clock, an iron, and a pair of ice skates—all in remarkably good condition after being packed away for more than sixty years.

There were portfolios of Margaret's papers, including her nursing diplomas from London and New York, student transcripts and evaluations, a handwritten résumé, her U.S. citizenship papers, and her will. She saved many greeting cards, postcards, and letters from friends, family, and co-workers, and collected maps, tourist brochures, and picture postcards from her travels. Among her belongings were hundreds of photographs of family and friends and of her many trips.

> 25682.124 ENVELOPE—*manila, one side completely torn open, full of post-cards, letters, assorted documentary materials*
> *Postcards, souvenir Folder (2) Saratoga Springs, NY and Halifax N.S. (1)*
> *(7) different postcards to D. from 1922 to 1940 various addresses. From friends traveling*
> *Map, large "Department of the Interior/ Canada/ Sectional Map/ Indicating Main/ Automobile Roads/ Between/ Canada & the United States/ Atlantic Sheet/ 1928" black pen line on Boston to Portland, Portland has been circled as has Halifax, Nova Scotia*
> *Photograph 3 x 5 black and white woman standing on porch of cabin #3, written in pencil on back "Overnight cabin, Waterbury August 1935" stamped 109 on back; negative number*

How did Margaret Dunleavy, an educated woman with a career and with close social connections, an independent woman who traveled widely and owned her own car in the 1930s, come to spend the last three decades of her life in a mental institution? Through papers found in her luggage and documents in her medical record—letters from family and former physicians, interviews with friends, her admission interview—it's possible to sort out some of the strands of her life experience that eventually brought her to Willard in 1941.

ORPHANED

Margaret's acquaintance with loss began early. Born in 1892 in Edinburgh, Scotland, she was the eldest daughter of a working-class couple. Her father, a merchant seaman, was struck in the chest by a steel cable while on a ship traveling the U.S. Great Lakes, which caused severe bleeding in his lungs. He blamed his ensuing tuberculosis on his weakened condition and the damp climate; he died of the disease when Margaret was just seven years old. Her mother, a widow at twenty-five, soon remarried. The children's paternal grandmother became concerned that Margaret and her younger sister Marie were not being well cared for, and contacted the Scottish National Society for the Prevention of Cruelty to Children, which determined that the girls' mother was neglectful and removed the children from her home. There are no records left to explain why the children were not taken in by relatives, or why their uncle sent the two little girls to an orphanage in Edinburgh. Their mother died shortly thereafter, although her estranged relatives did not recall the cause of her death.

Before her tenth birthday, Margaret had experienced the death of her father, the punitive removal from her home under allegations of neglect, her mother's subsequent death, and abandonment by her remaining family to a stark life in an orphanage. The long-closed institution did not yield any records that might shed light on the time the sisters spent there, but certainly an Edinburgh orphanage at the turn of the twentieth century was not a nurturing place. In her history of similar institutions, *The Orphan Country*, Lynn Abrams describes the atmosphere:

> The orphanage routine was designed to prepare children for life after care . . . which was assumed to be domestic service for the girls and farm service or manual labor for the boys. . . . The regimentation, household chores and the routine of residential life all combined to create a disciplinary environment for children who had committed no crime. . . . What would today be regarded as random and unnecessary violence—usually strokes from the strap or the cane—were regularly inflicted for a wide variety of petty misdemeanours from failing to learn a psalm by heart . . . to behaviours that should have been dealt with sympathetically, such as bed-wetting and running away.

"We were more or less treated as a 'herd,' not as individuals" was one woman's recollection of treatment in the orphanage. The lack of individual loving attention inherent in institutional settings and the resulting emotional deprivation often carried lifelong repercussions for those confined there.

An ongoing study begun in the 1980s by the Centers for Disease Control on the lifelong impact of a range of childhood traumas may shed further light on how Margaret Dunleavy's very difficult childhood might have contributed to her later ill health and psychological distress. The Adverse Child Experiences (ACE) study examined nearly eighteen thousand individuals and found that exposure to even one category of adverse childhood events had a strong correlation with poor physical health and/or emotional well-being in adults. For women like Margaret, who were exposed to several categories of adverse experiences, the risks rose exponentially.

With her history of childhood deprivation, neglect, and loss, it says something for the strength of Margaret's character and the resilience of her nature that she took the initiative to leave the orphanage at age sixteen, finding work as a nanny. Years later, Margaret's aunt, Edith Dunleavy, wrote to the superintendent of Willard State Hospital in response to a query about the family's history. Her letter described sixteen-year-old Margaret as "an exceptionally bright and happy girl," adding, "Our home was always open to her and she came a great deal to it." Margaret apparently never told even her closest friends of her years in the orphanage; when Willard doctors questioned her friends in 1941, they all stated that Aunt Edith had raised Margaret and her sister.

BECOMING A CAREGIVER

In 1912, the family for whom she worked moved to London, and twenty-year-old Margaret went along. "After a time," Edith wrote, "she desired to better her position. I suggested she should take up hospital nursing as I thought she was adapted to it, being of a bright, kindly disposition, very practical, and possessing a sound common sense."

Margaret Dunleavy enrolled in nurse's training at London's North East Metropolitan Hospital in August 1916. She befriended a fellow student, a native Londoner named Florence Smith, who would remain a lifelong friend. After completing her training in July 1918, she was hired as a probationary nurse. Her work there was deemed "very satisfactory," and she was promoted to staff nurse in February 1919, and worked there until she left for the United States in August 1921.

During her early years of study and nursing, daily life in London was often disrupted by the ongoing World War. Food rationing became necessary and German air attacks put civilians directly in harm's way. Margaret was dealt yet another series of blows: "The hospital suffered air raids in the war," according to Aunt Edith, "and her fiancé was killed in France, within a few weeks of going to the front."

In 1921, Miss Dunleavy emigrated to the United States, sailing alone from Liverpool on the SS *Caronia*, and arrived in New York City, where she found work as a private duty nurse. For a young working-class woman of her time, making such a major change in her life took great determination. But the reasons for her decision to leave Great Britain remain unclear; unlike many immigrants of the time, she had ample opportunities to make a good living at home. Perhaps she wanted to put all those losses and deprivations behind her and start afresh. Her nursing school friend Florence Smith moved to the United States in 1918 and may have encouraged Margaret to follow. Her ambitions hampered by the strict class distinctions of Edwardian England, tales of the possibilities open to hardworking immigrants may have lured her to America.

"My husband," Aunt Edith wrote, "[was concerned about Margaret's move] because she was actually going to the very part [of America] her father blamed for his ill health and Margaret had a tendency to nasal

catarrh and head colds. We also felt her nursing experience was quite inadequate to make her way in a strange country. I suggested she should take a year of general nursing in a private nursing home and also qualify in midwifery but Margaret did not think that was necessary."

After two years of private duty nursing in New York, Margaret apparently did feel the need for more training, and enrolled in a graduate course in obstetrics at Woman's Hospital of New York State. Again, she got good marks on "character, tact and adaptability," and her teachers felt that she presented "a very dignified professional appearance, worked very hard and tried to progress." After completing her coursework, she was hired by the hospital as a general duty nurse, and the quality of her work was deemed "excellent." But her evaluation also described her as "very nervous and self-conscious" and "conscientious, but extremely reticent."

Margaret, Woman's Hospital, New York, 1924

This photo found among her belongings shows Miss Dunleavy in her nurse's uniform sitting calmly and erect in front of the New York City skyline. This is just the kind of picture a young immigrant might send to relatives back home, showing that she had succeeded in America: all prim, formal, and shyly proud, seated near windows with those famed skyscrapers in the background.

INJURY AND ILLNESS

Tragedy was never far from success for Margaret Dunleavy. While training at Woman's Hospital, she slipped on a wet concrete floor, injured her head, and took weeks to recuperate. A physician who treated her later in life described the aftermath: "She suffered with traumatic nervousness for about nine months after this," and had "frequent severe headaches" for years afterward. The head injury was the first in a series of serious health problems that Margaret experienced during her thirties. Aunt Edith, writing in 1941 to Willard superintendent Dr. Kenneth Keill, lamented that "since leaving this country [Scotland], Margaret has suffered misfortune after misfortune."

She worked at Woman's Hospital for a year after completing her training, when, in an eerie echoing of her father's life, Margaret had severe bleeding of the lungs and was diagnosed with tuberculosis. Admitted to the Loomis Sanatorium in New York's Catskill Mountains in 1925, she was diagnosed with "moderately advanced pulmonary tuberculosis . . . (and) had symptoms strongly suggestive of enteric [gastrointestinal] tuberculosis," according to the medical chief of staff. Before antibiotic treatment, gastrointestinal tuberculosis was a serious and incurable condition, and its painful symptoms overshadowed the rest of her life. Curiously, despite this clear-cut history, her severe abdominal pain was often considered psychosomatic by doctors she encountered. In many ways, tuberculosis came to define the trajectory of Miss Dunleavy's personal and professional life; the constant stressors of the disease compounded other issues in her life, leaving her more susceptible to the emotional distress that led to her eventual commitment to Willard. She remained at the sanatorium for almost eighteen months; during that time, her nine-year-old nephew died suddenly in Scotland, and Margaret took this news very hard. When she was finally discharged in January 1926, she was referred to a specialist in New York City for treatment of her gastrointestinal condition.

But she did not return to New York City, most likely because she had no place to go. Since she had lived in the nurses' residence at Woman's Hospital and lost her job due to illness, she was essentially homeless. Instead, she went to stay with her friend Jessie Cole in Buffalo. But less than a month after her discharge from the sanatorium, Margaret was admitted to a TB hospital in Perrysburg, New York, with active pulmonary tuberculosis.

She spent three and a half years at Perrysburg, bringing the total length of her hospitalization for tuberculosis to five years. The TB she contracted in the line of duty deprived her of a nursing career at a prestigious New York hospital and isolated her from her circle of woman friends. She corresponded regularly with Jessie Cole, Aunt Edith, and her sister Marie, who had become a nurse in Edinburgh. Florence Smith, her friend from nursing school, married a man from upstate New York, and the couple became frequent correspondents and occasional visitors. But despite the letters, Margaret Dunleavy was still alone and sick in a foreign country, with few resources, and with an ever heavier burden of hardship and ill health.

SECRET ROMANCE

At Perrysburg, she developed a strong tie to a fellow patient of Scottish descent, Arthur Dargavell, a widower twelve years her senior. Their relationship seems to have sustained her during her long stay in the sanatorium. Margaret denied that they had a romantic relationship, claiming that they

Margaret and Arthur with unidentified woman in wheelchair, c. 1932

stayed in adjoining rooms on the weekend trips they took together in the years after leaving the sanatorium. Mr. Dargavell's daughter, Hazel Merriman, considered their relationship merely "one of convenience," denying any romantic attachment.

But it was quite likely that Arthur and Margaret were secret lovers; certainly they had a close, long-standing relationship that was important to both of them. Margaret often visited with Arthur's extended family, and in the sixteen years between their meeting at the sanatorium and Margaret's admission to Willard, the two saw a great deal of each other. Arthur stayed faithful to Margaret even after her commitment, visiting her frequently during her first few years at Willard. Margaret usually spent Christmas with Arthur, whom she had nicknamed "Dar." Photos of the two found in her suitcase show a tall, slim, well-dressed white-haired man standing next to a short, solidly built woman with a broad, open face, somewhat conservatively dressed, her hair in a bun. The seriousness of their relationship is evident in the will that Margaret left behind.

231.4a,b a—Document, *Will/* of */Margaret D. / Dated July 12th 1935.*
Last Will and Testament/ I, Margaret D., of the/city of Buffalo, in the County of Erie County and State of New York, being of sound mind and memory, do make, publish and declare this my last Will and Testament, in manner following, that is to say: First, I direct that all my debts and funeral expenses be paid. Second, I hereby bequest my car to be given to A D. Dargavell & all money left after my debts are paid and all my personal effects/ Lastly, I hereby appoint Arthur D Dargavell executor of this, my last will and testament, hereby revoking all former wills by me any time

made; and I give my said executor full power and authority to lease, mort-gage, or sell and convey any and all of my real property as fully as I might do living.

In Witness Whereof, I have here unto set my hand at Buffalo, Erie County, N.Y., this day of July 12th, 1935/ Margaret D.

Arthur, too, demonstrated his commitment to Margaret in a letter written on a lined yellow legal pad at one A.M. in February 1941:

Dear Marge/ this is the only paper I have handy. Your/ letter arrived O.K. and I sure was glad to get it/ You surely are having a regular time of/ it with all the doctors you are seeing./ Hope they do you some good. I was/ especially glad to hear that your head was/ not going to bother you. It must be a / relief for you to have that worry over/ with. . . . This week it has/ been very cold but clear. I renewed your paper/ today. So you can read the Lackawanna News / I feel fine right now and that is some thing/ as I will confess now that I have been worried/ for 2 years thinking I was losing my mind./ Those head aches were terrible and they/ come right back if I get too tired. It will be fine/ if we can both feel better this summer. I feel/ sure I will when the weather is better. That/ was a nice Valentine and made me very happy/ I will write again soon/ Love always/ Dar

Ironically, this letter, with its implications for a better and healthier future together, was posted just four months before Margaret Dunleavy disappeared behind Willard's locked doors. She was not the only woman whose sexuality was suppressed once she entered Willard. In those days, there was little reference to such matters, but if one combs through the records carefully, one can find hints that women expressed sexual desires but were thwarted by the institutional regime. In Margaret's case, she had to give up her most important relationship to a man when she entered Willard. This fact must have contributed to the unremitting despondency documented in her hospital records.

AN OCEANSIDE REFUGE

After her discharge from Perrysburg in 1929, Margaret stayed for a while with friends in Ocean Grove, New Jersey. Photographs and souvenir postcard packets of the Jersey shore were found in Margaret's belongings. Apparently, her friends' oceanfront home made a lasting impression upon her; nearly forty years later, Margaret implored the Willard staff to let her return "home" to Ocean Grove, facing the Atlantic.

Margaret Dunleavy's handwritten résumé shows that after leaving the sanitorium, she did private-duty nursing in Buffalo, where she stayed at

Jessie Cole's home. In October 1930, she became a naturalized U.S. citizen. She kept in touch with colleagues from Woman's Hospital and turned to them for help in finding private nursing positions. Although Margaret was described by several acquaintances as quiet, even seclusive, she inspired real loyalty among her close friends. Hazel Merriman noted that "Her circle of friends has always been small but very devoted to her, and rightly so, as she is a woman to be admired, easy to entertain, and pleased with so little." She goes on to say that Margaret's "quiet disposition made her an ideal companion for my father, who talks all the time." Both Jessie Cole and Florence Smith wrote to her and often visited during her early years at Willard; they continued to send clothing and other personal items for years afterward, despite Margaret's reluctance or inability to answer their letters. They wrote frequently to Superintendent Keill, inquiring about her condition and reminding him that she had friends outside who cared about her.

INTREPID MOTORIST

In 1931, Margaret Dunleavy took a nursing job at Newton Memorial Hospital, a TB facility in Cassadaga, New York, where she worked until 1936. These years seem to have been stable, happy and productive ones for her. An accomplished seamstress, she made most of her own clothes, and was adept at embroidery, knitting, and crochet. Her trunks were filled with a variety of needlework, along with an assortment of sewing notions, paper patterns, knitting books, fabric, and embroidery materials. There were two heavily embroidered tablecloths, one unfinished with the needle and embroidery thread still in the fabric. Among the clothing she made were hand-sewn silk, rayon, and cotton dresses, including a navy blue polka-dot dress and jacket that Margaret wears in several photographs found in her trunk.

With a steady income again, Margaret bought a used car, a 1929 Ford, which allowed her to visit her friends across New York State. Arthur Dargavell lived with his daughter in Binghamton, almost three hundred miles and a day's drive from Cassadaga. Margaret's friend from London, Florence Smith, lived ninety-five miles away, and Jessie Cole was in Buffalo, a fifty-five-mile trip. Automobile journeys across such distances were still something of an adventure in the early 1930s, particularly for a woman traveling alone, but she seemed to have a passion for driving. She took vacation trips by car every summer, in addition to weekend trips with Arthur Dargavell. Margaret's car was clearly her ticket to freedom and a way to connect with her far-flung friends.

Her resolute traveling spirit is illustrated by a trip she took in August 1936. Setting out from Cassadaga with Jessie and Flo, she drove through

Flo, Jessie, and Margaret en route to Nova Scotia, 1936

the Adirondacks, the Green Mountains of Vermont, the White Mountains of New Hampshire, and up the coast of Maine. When the three women finally arrived in Chester, Nova Scotia, Margaret was reunited with her sister, Marie, who had come from Scotland to spend the summer as a nanny in this wealthy seaside resort. This was the first face-to-face meeting between the two sisters since Margaret moved to the United States, and it would turn out to be their last.

The photos show a relaxed summer road trip and a happy family reunion. The very normalcy of these pictures—they could have been snapped by any group of tourists making a similar trip around the same time— seems ironic in light of the events that occurred just a few years later. Nothing in these photos foreshadows the dire turn that Margaret's life was about to take.

THE BODY IS TALKING

Contrary to the picture of health she portrays in the snapshots, Margaret Dunleavy was plagued with health problems during the years she worked in Cassadaga. One wonders how she managed to work full-time and keep up with her friends and her travels while dealing with so much ill health. Unlike conditions that were considered "hysterical" (later called "somatization disorder"), Margaret had easily identifiable causes in her medical history, and undoubtedly "real" symptoms, although some doctors she encountered over the years saw her as hypochondriacal. For eleven years she was under the care of Dr. A. H. Garvin in Buffalo. He gave her highly potent (and to some extent, addictive) drugs, including belladonna, codeine syrup, and endocrine products, all of which may cause psychiatric and neurological symptoms. Her continuing health problems, which failed to respond to the treatments of the time, made her more vulnerable to stress.

In 1937, Margaret Dunleavy took a position as a staff nurse at Herman Biggs Memorial Hospital in Ithaca, a well known TB facility. This move put her much closer to Arthur Dargavell, who lived just an hour's drive away. Margaret worked at Biggs Hospital up until the day she was admitted to Willard in 1941.

WOUNDED HEALER

Biggs Memorial Hospital occupied a sprawling rural campus just north of Ithaca on the western shore of Cayuga Lake. Most nurses lived in a residence on the grounds, giving them easy access to Ithaca and the Cornell University campus across the lake. Margaret likely took advantage of these opportunities; a map of the Cornell campus and a brochure of its art museum were found among her papers. She seems to have developed warm relationships with her TB patients; there are photographs of Margaret in uniform posing with smiling patients in robes and wheelchairs on the hospital's expansive porches. If this was a happy period in Margaret's life, as the photos seem to indicate, it didn't last very long.

Margaret Dunleavy and TB patient, Biggs Memorial Hospital, Ithaca, New York, c. 1938

But Margaret was far from giving up on herself and her career. She decided to pursue state licensure as a nurse, buying exam preparation books in a variety of specialties. The process of getting her license was mired with obstacles and setbacks, and troubled her right up until her arrival at Willard. This nagging unfinished business was likely one of the many stressful factors that led to her institutionalization.

With the outbreak of World War II, Margaret expressed increasing worry about the safety of her family in Scotland. Her aunt and sister were in Edinburgh, directly across the Firth of Forth from the site of the first German air attack on Great Britain. On October 16, 1939, Luftwaffe planes bombed the Royal Naval Base at Rosyth, and Edinburgh sustained damage in the resulting air battle. Civilian areas of the city were also bombed on several occasions. Knowing that her family members were in harm's way, along with the slow pace of the foreign mail, took a toll on Margaret's peace of mind.

DISCONTINUITY OF CARE

Margaret's health worsened between 1939 and 1941, compounding the stress of the war and her frustrating efforts to get a nursing license. Despite the distance, she continued to see Dr. Garvin in Buffalo; she must have placed great confidence in him to make such a long trip. Possibly, she continued to see him because he prescribed certain remedies she could not easily obtain elsewhere. In early 1939, Margaret Dunleavy was hospitalized with an upper respiratory infection. Through the following year her abdominal pain was unrelenting, but no surgically amenable causes could be found. She was admitted to Buffalo General Hospital for more tests and radium treatments.

Her superiors at Biggs Hospital decided to intervene, as they apparently felt that her decision to consult a physician 150 miles away was a sign of bad judgment. Explaining his position in a letter to Superintendent Keill, Dr. John K. Deegan, the superintendent at Biggs, wrote: "In January 1941 the entire situation was gone over with Miss D. and it was decided that a local physician might give her more relief than a physician as far away as Buffalo. Miss D. was given a choice between a hospital attending doctor or a local private practitioner. At her request she was referred to Dr. Wallace who took over her care at that time until June 1941 when she was referred to Willard." Losing a relationship with one's long-standing doctor would have a negative impact on any patient, but especially so for Margaret, who experienced so many chronic medical problems that did not seem curable. If Dr. Garvin sustained her with personal support and remedies that ameliorated her suffering, his loss might have been the single event that tipped the scales, transforming Margaret from a working woman with many serious physical ailments to an institutionalized mental patient.

THE UNRAVELING

We can begin to see the how the escalating combination of stresses she experienced in the months preceding her admission made Margaret Dunleavy feel "like a fly in a spider web." She was in constant physical pain when her supervisors took the drastic step of disrupting her relationship with her doctor. At the same time, she was experiencing problems with people at work. She felt the dieticians were resentful of having to prepare the special meals that had been ordered for her. There was gossip about Margaret's relationship with Arthur Dargavell. The hospital had no private telephone booths, and staff could easily eavesdrop on one another's personal calls; Margaret's overheard conversations with Arthur became grist for the rumor mill. She continued to worry about her family in Scotland, according to her friends, and especially her nephew Richard, serving in the Royal Air Force in South Africa.

With the quest for a nursing license still dragging on after four years, due to essential papers from London that never arrived, Margaret began to wonder if hospital administrators were keeping these documents from her. From her perspective, she had reasons not to trust them after they intervened so inappropriately in her medical care. In the midst of these escalating worries, Arthur Dargavell had a heart attack, and Margaret, at first believing he had died, felt responsible for this calamity, due to the hospital gossip about their relationship. By this time, her emotional state must have been quite desperate, and events beyond her control must have seemed overwhelming.

One way of understanding Miss Dunleavy's situation is to see her expressions of anguish as a "narrative of chaos." In his book *The Wounded Storyteller*, Arthur W. Frank describes the need of people who are sick to tell their stories in order to regain control of their relationships with their own bodies. While Frank writes about physical illnesses, his insights are easily applicable to emotional distress. He proposes three types of illness narratives: the restitution narrative (Yesterday I was healthy, today I am sick, tomorrow I'll be healthy again); the chaos narrative (Life is overwhelming and will never get better); and the quest narrative (I accept that my life will never be the same—what can I learn from this?).

The chaos narrative is essentially an anti-narrative, because the self in the midst of chaos has no time for reflection or the ordering of narrative in a way that makes meaning. As Frank puts it, "A person who has recently started to experience pain speaks of 'it' hurting 'me' and can dissociate from 'it.' The chaos narrative is lived when 'it' has hammered 'me' out of self-recognition." Chaos stories are hard to hear, both literally, because, in their lack of sequence and causality, they may not be apparent as stories to the listener, and figuratively, because they are anxiety-producing, even threatening, to the listener, a reminder that anyone of us may find herself in this painful state.

These were the circumstances of Margaret Dunleavy's life in June 1941, when Dr. Wallace observed that "Miss D. had increasing feelings of persecution. These finally became so severe that it was felt no longer safe for her to work as a nurse at this hospital." Although she had no prior psychiatric history, Dr. Wallace recommended that Margaret be sent to Willard State Hospital instead of first referring her for outpatient psychiatric care.

The doctor who saw Margaret at her admission noted that she "was pleasant, agreeable, and correctly oriented" and that she "almost completely denied the statements made about her in the health officer's certificate." He went on to say that "She further denies auditory and visual hallucinations. . . . The reason for hospitalization was explained to her." Significantly, the doctor did not make a note of the explanation he gave Margaret for her admission.

Despite her denials of hallucinations, and the rather threadbare evidence, even under the loose standards of those days, Miss Dunleavy was promptly diagnosed with "Dementia Praecox, Paranoid" (now called schizophrenia). She had no psychiatric history, and most certainly did not meet the criteria for that diagnosis. If anything, she suffered a crisis precipitated by the sudden illness of Arthur Dargavell, aggravated by stress about her

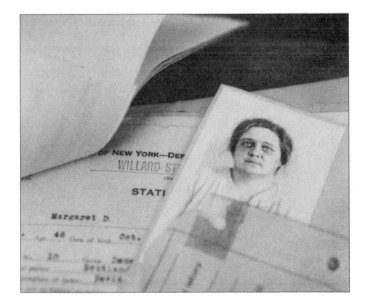

nursing license, personal problems at work, worries about her family's wartime safety, and her chronic health problems, for which there were no effective treatments. Add to this list of stressors the loss of her personal physician due to the meddling of her employer, and we can see how vulnerable Margaret must have become to any perceived slight, especially from her co-workers and employer.

When the doors slammed shut behind her at Willard, Margaret found herself completely engulfed. A note in her chart on the day of her admission states that she "seems to be at a complete loss as to why she was brought here. . . . Patient does not believe herself mentally ill." Margaret Dunleavy had spent the majority of her life in institutions, either as an inmate or a caregiver—from her childhood in the orphanage, through her nursing training and work in London and the United States, as a TB patient in two different facilities, and later as a TB nurse in three others. Previously, she had found ways to compensate for the regimentation of living and working in hospitals, through the emotional support of friends and family, her car trips, and her general industriousness. But this time the institutionalization was ominous and final. As we have seen with the stories of other suitcase owners, the psychiatric staff did not attempt to make connections between their newly admitted patients' distress and their life circumstances.

DECADES ON A LOCKED WARD

MARGARET D. #25682
OCTOBER 3, 1941:   SUMMARY PRESENTATION
Presented by Dr. Howard in conference with Dr. Kilpatrick

This is an extremely interesting case which has been seen by many individuals, so that we have a record of her acute difficulty which is thoroughly complete. There is lacking however, a record of her early development. Her reaction has been characterized by a gradual developing paranoid reaction over a period of years. It is true that her acute difficulty resulted in commitment fairly recently; however, it is my clinical impression that we are dealing with a case of Dementia Praecox of long duration. It is interesting that when she took the Post Graduate course many years ago she was noted as, "peculiar, temperamental, supersensitive, extremely reticent and nervous." The climacteric [menopause] undoubtedly has some influence on the picture at the present time. It seems reasonably definite that we are dealing with a case of schizophrenia.

DIAGNOSIS: 18—DEMENTIA PRAECOX, *Paranoid*
                                        —*C. A. Kilpatrick, M.D., Acting Clinical Director*

To Drs. Kilpatrick and Howard, Miss Dunleavy became a "case" and was discussed as an object. While they were aware of the precipitating incidents through interviews with her friends, the doctors gave no credence to the impact of these stressors on her mental and emotional state (although they did assume that menopause was an exacerbating factor). Instead, they quoted fifteen-year-old employment evaluations to support their "clinical impression" that Margaret was "a case of Dementia Praecox of long duration."

Once placed on a locked ward, Margaret's mental state deteriorated quickly. Barely a week after her admission, the record states that "She admits being hallucinated, and states she hears various people, but is unable to distinguish their voices." Not infrequently, someone who is in crisis, but has never been hospitalized before, starts experiencing more extreme symptoms once she finds herself confined in the company of other patients in varying states of emotional alienation. It's also possible that she was experiencing withdrawal symptoms from the powerful drugs she had been taking, which were discontinued once she entered Willard.

After a month on the ward, she remained "depressed and hallucinated." Six months after her admission, a psychiatrist stated, "This patient is definitely paranoid in her thinking and expresses delusional ideas about her commitment and detention here. Patient appears preoccupied, refuses to do any work, and spends most of her time in idleness." Over the next thirty-two years, there is little variation in the notes in her chart, except that Margaret was put on heavy doses of Thorazine beginning in the 1960s, and doctor's notes were written less frequently as the years passed.

SEPTEMBER 2, 1942: *PARANOID, SECLUSIVE, NO INSIGHT, PHYSICALLY WELL*

This patient continues paranoid and is evidently hallucinated although she denies hearing voices. She is asocial. She lacks insight, judgment is poor, and she feels she should be released from the hospital. Her general physical condition appears satisfactory.

—Dr. W. Strong

APRIL 28, 1947: *[Last note February 14, 1946]*

This patient is cooperative, pleasant, and docile but has elaborate delusions, and states that the examiner will be tried and sentenced for daring to examine her. —Dr. Bull

AUGUST 21, 1952: *SILLY, HALLUCINATED*

This patient is at times incoherent and markedly irrelevant. She was very hostile during the interview but lacked appropriate emotion. She was quite silly, proceeding to clear her throat again and again. She is markedly hallucinated. —Dr. Walker

MAY 1, 1969: *PROGRESS NOTE*

This patient has shown no change in her mental condition. She is still somewhat withdrawn and delusional. She is inappropriate in her affect. Judgment continues to be impaired. —James M. Jennings, M.D.

If Margaret Dunleavy had received a different kind of treatment than the neglectful warehousing offered her, might her life have turned out differently? Arthur Frank's work suggests the possibility that, had Margaret's chaos narrative been listened to empathetically, the crisis that sent her to Willard might have constituted an interruption in her life story, rather than a mute downward spiral:

> The need to honor chaos stories is both moral and clinical. . . . To deny a chaos story is to deny the person telling this story, and people who are being denied cannot be cared for. People whose reality is denied can remain recipients of treatments and services, but they cannot be participants in empathic relations of care.

But occasionally, there were moments of connection with the staff. As a young, newly graduated nurse, Donna Gustafson Cerza took care of Margaret during the last months of her life. Margaret was very ill; she had diabetes, congestive heart failure, and surgeries for a bowel obstruction and for gallstones. While she remained largely silent, she made a strong impression on Ms. Cerza, who vividly recalled caring for her thirty-two years later.

DP: *Donna, you mentioned that you took care of Margaret when she was an elderly woman. Can you tell us what you remember?*

DC: *My first recollection, after I saw the picture of her, entering the exhibit (at the New York State Museum), was as a new graduate nurse. . . . Margaret had abdominal surgery and was doing her post-op care in Elliot Hall on the Willard State Hospital grounds.*

DP: *And what year was that?*

DC: *It had to be . . . probably between June of 1972 and November of 1973.*

DP: *What do you remember of her personality? What kind of woman was she?*

DC: *Oh, she was a very sweet lady. She was a quiet, gentle spirit.... If I would go to bring her medicine or get her a drink or take her temperature, blood pressure, whatever, she was always very cooperative. Even if she had discomfort, she didn't complain.*

DP: *Did she talk at all about herself, or her past, when you knew her?*

DC: *No, she really did not. She would answer questions posed to her. She would listen to us when we would share a story with her. She would listen and she would make eye contact, but she really didn't converse a lot. I would hug her. She would hug me back, and she was a very quiet, gentle spirit.*

7.
HOW PEOPLE WERE TREATED AT WILLARD

The history of medicine is, in effect, the history of discarded therapies.

—GERALD GROB, medical historian

Willard was a bustling, self-contained community with plenty of activity, but it offered very little that could be called mental health treatment during its first seventy-five years. As reflected in the life story of Lawrence Marek, the grave digger, it was unique among early asylums because it was seen as a last resort for people who were never expected to recover. The doctors who established Willard believed that while treatment was futile, the "incurables" were perfectly capable of providing a major share of the work necessary to run the place of their confinement. Dorothea Dix and other reformers who campaigned to create state asylums that provided moral treatment for all who might benefit would have been horrified at the eventual results of their efforts: large, impersonal institutions that did not provide inmates with treatment that even vaguely resembled the compassionate approach of the Quakers.

Willard essentially provided custodial care: food, shelter, and (sometimes) clothing. In the early years, the families of patients who were not destitute were expected to supply clothing and personal-care items, as well as a monthly stipend for room and board. People admitted to Willard were not classified mainly by diagnosis, but according to their ability to work. Even if patient labor was portrayed as therapeutic by the doctors, its primary purpose was to sustain the institution while keeping the patients occupied. Those considered violent or unable to take care of themselves were kept in locked "back wards," where life was very regimented and boring. These wards were feared for their filth, lack of heat, and neglect. Everyone else was expected, and strongly encouraged, to work.

Sewing room, c. 1890

Shoemaking shop, c. 1890

Farm labor, c. 1910

Road work, c. 1900

One of the more industrious patients at Willard, Fred Towner, kept a diary in which he recorded his daily activities for at least five consecutive months in 1926. Towner did all manner of things to keep himself busy and to earn some money. He also had a considerable amount of freedom, riding the train to various stations around Seneca Lake, picking up newspapers, telegrams, and merchandise, and delivering them for a fee to a fair number of customers. Most of his days were similar:

TUESDAY, JANUARY 5, 1926
Arose, eat breakfast, sit around a little while. Then help saw some wood for the fireplace. Went after the mail returned eat dinner. Sit around and read a while. I have enough money collected in to pay for December papers 10.85 and mailed remittance this afternoon. Eat supper, sit around and read until bedtime. Went to bed.

SUNDAY, MARCH 21, 1926
Arose, made my bed, washed, eat breakfast, got ready and walked to Gilbert [train depot] *after the Sunday Elmira Telegrams, sold 41 papers, ate dinner, went north and sold 25 more papers. Ate supper, smoked, went to bed.*

Every Monday night he went to the picture show.

Medical Care

Willard did provide its patients with physical health care. The founders had vastly underestimated the need for these services, and a small infirmary was built to care for people arriving from county poorhouses, many of whom suffered from medical problems that had remained untreated for years. Since insanity in women was often assumed to be related to "female" problems, Willard hired its first woman physician in 1885. Her primary role was to give gynecological exams and keep extensive records on the problems of women patients. In a fourteen-month period, she examined 389 women, and found that only four of them had "normal" reproductive organs. Despite recording these problems, the doctor provided almost no treatment for conditions like fibroid tumors or prolapsed uteruses. Many women were embarrassed about the examinations and some resisted fiercely; examinations were sometimes carried out by force. No matter what medical condition a woman presented with—tuberculosis, heart problems, respiratory distress—she was subjected to a gynecological exam.

With large numbers of people confined in close quarters, infection was always a concern, and Willard doctors had to cope with outbreaks of influenza, tuberculosis, diphtheria and typhoid fever over the decades. Nancy Jaycot Caniff, an occupational therapist at Willard from 1959 to 1989, describes the plight of typhoid patients kept in isolation in 1959:

> The typhoid patients . . . I think there were four of them and they were located in Edgemere and they lived in what I call a cage. It was a long wire cage and they used to pass their lunch in and they weren't ever allowed out. They passed their food through a little box and they brought the dishes out and took care of them specially. They had no activities at all. They just kind of sat around in that cage all day long. Their beds were in there. They each had a chair and . . . all I can remember them being dressed in is white slips. I don't recall them being in dresses or anything.

Aside from periodic outbreaks of contagious diseases, which greatly taxed the facility and caused many deaths, medical care became increasingly important as the population started to age. Without the deadly complications of the new psychotropic medications—obesity, cardiovascular disease, and diabetes—and with a diet consisting mostly of farm-fresh products, the population at Willard had a chance to live a long life within the confines of the institution. Even those who suffered from serious illnesses, like Ethel and Margaret, were apparently treated well enough to live with their conditions for a good many years. The medical units may have offered more humane care than the general psychiatric wards.

ENTERTAINMENT AND RECREATION

From the beginning, Willard offered recreation and entertainment to patients who were allowed to leave their wards. Entertainment was considered "therapeutic," but in fact was primarily designed to lighten the workload of the attendants and administrators. Marching drills, calisthenics, basketball, and baseball took place on a weekly basis. The annual Field Days, with races, tug-of-war, exhibits of goods manufactured in the shops on the hospital grounds, livestock competitions, and other outdoor activities for the amusement of patients, staff, and local spectators, often drew over fifteen hundred attendees. In 1893, Hadley Hall was built, with a five-hundred-seat auditorium and a bowling alley. Dances were held there, along with concerts, lectures, and amateur theatrics. Starting in the 1920s, Hadley Hall was used for Monday night screenings of films like *Spook Ranch*, *Love Hour*, *The Siege*, and *The Iron Horse*, which were quite popular among patients, staff, and their families. Entertainment was not part of the hospital's budget and Willard superintendents raised money from local businesses and individual donors.

The stage at Hadley Hall, c. 1910

OCCUPATIONAL THERAPY AND REHABILITATION

Occupational therapy (OT), first developed in the United States in 1914, was introduced at Willard in the early 1920s. When the term was used in the early to mid twentieth century to describe work done with mental patients, "occupational" referred to "being occupied" rather than to preparing for a career, as one might think. Art and craft activities were the primary "therapies" offered, including weaving, rug-making, leather work, basketry, needlework, light woodwork, drawing, painting, and pottery making.

For many patients, occupational therapy was an opportunity to get away from the boredom of the ward routine, have an opportunity to social- ize, and to distract themselves from their emotional distress or despair. Nancy Jaycot Caniff describes Margaret Dunleavy's response to OT:

> *I did OT with Margaret in Sunnycroft. She just kind of sat and she liked to talk. She really didn't participate that much. She just liked to be in the group and she liked to talk and she liked to go out on trips and things like that. We did community trips, chitchatted and talked about everyday things.*

For a few patients, like Dmytre Zarchuck, who discovered that he had a talent for painting, OT opened up new vistas, bringing new meaning to life despite their institutionalization.

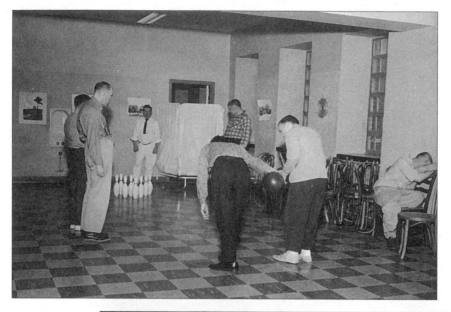

Occupational Therapy, c. 1960

In the 1970s, OT activities turned to more practical matters as large numbers of patients were prepared for release. When asked what kind of activities were done in OT with patients, Nancy Jaycot Caniff responded: "This was before you did any group therapy with them. In the beginning, it was mainly arts and crafts—painting, sewing, ceramics—things like that. And then, probably in the seventies, we went into on-the-job training. We did accounting and typing and things like that trying to get them ready to go outside."

Willard opened the state system's first Rehabilitation Department, which offered groups to teach socialization skills and what were referred to as "activities of daily living": cooking, shopping, budgeting, grooming, and the like. A halfway house was opened on the grounds for people who were in their final months of preparation to leave the facility. There was a sheltered workshop where patients did piecework and were paid according to the work they accomplished rather than with an hourly wage.

MENTAL HEALTH TREATMENTS

Before the introduction of "modern" psychiatric drugs in the 1950s, there was little offered in the way of mental health treatment, with a few notable exceptions. Hydrotherapy, where people were submerged and confined for long periods of time in cold or tepid baths, was quite different from the balneotherapy that wealthy people enjoyed in spas around the world. Mainly designed to calm unruly and agitated patients, it was an ordeal championed by doctors that even the orderlies tended to dread. Insulin and Metrazol shock "treatment" were introduced in 1937, both designed to induce violent seizures; these were replaced a few years later by electroshock "therapy." The jolts that were supposed to tear people out of various altered states quickly became known for their brutality and the way they wiped out memories, sometimes entire periods of a life. Nevertheless, Willard doctors administered 1,443 shock "treatments" in 1942 alone. Lobotomy, the most infamous of all modern "psychiatric treatments," was never performed at Willard, although people who had been subjected to this iatrogenic brain damage at other New York State facilities were sometimes transferred there.

Jessica was born at Willard in 1946 when her mother was hospitalized there; as a young adult, she was also committed to Willard. In 2001, she was interviewed by Jeanne Dumont, Ph.D., an ex-patient researcher, and recalled her mother's reaction to the treatment she received at Willard:

Q. *When you were young, did you go to visit her at Willard?*

A. *Yeah, a few times that I recall. I remember the first time I visited Willard. It was a stormy day and when we got there I got kind of scared by the big ancient buildings. . . . I must have been around seven or eight years old. And after that I always had a scary feeling about Willard from the times my mother was there, because she hated it so much. She just fought going there.*

Q. *Could you talk a little bit more about that? Did your mom say what it was about Willard, why she hated it so?*

A. *The main thing she hated—and was scared of—was the shock treatments. She had many of them. She often talked about how awful they were and how terrible she felt after she had them. They also did something back then that they called "cold packs," where they wrapped her up in wet sheets and set her in a tub with ice. Oh, dear, she hated that, too. So, I would say it was mainly the treatments she got there that she hated. Another treatment they gave her was insulin shock treatment. From what she described, they gave her insulin to the point where she went into a coma and that was very unpleasant, of course. She became diabetic when she was older and I often wondered if that had something to do with it. She described spending all day sitting on benches in the day room, and it just all sounded pretty awful to me.*

Q. *That was in the forties?*

A. *Forties and fifties, yeah.*

The introduction of neuroleptic drugs like Thorazine in the mid-1950s helped staff control patients who were crammed into ever-tighter quarters, but the medical charts offer little evidence that the drugs actually improved people's mental or emotional states. They merely subdued them and made them more tractable. The term *neuroleptic*, adopted from the Greek, means to "take hold of the nervous system," and, indeed, used in high doses, the drugs essentially served as chemical restraints. The doctors who first used such drugs never assumed that people would recover sufficiently to be released. They were simply looking for ways to handle large numbers of troubled (or troublesome) people as efficiently as possible. More than two decades after their first use, these drugs were cited as the first step in the massive downsizing of state hospitals that became known as deinstitutionalization, even though this was essentially a political and financial decision implemented by fiat from above. By 1955, neuroleptic drugs were in wide use in state mental hospitals across the country, including at Willard. The fact that they often caused severe neurological reactions like Parkinsonism and powerful muscle spasms was taken by the psychiatrists of the time as a signal that the drugs were effective. But the real effect of Thorazine and similar drugs was to create the kind of quiet hopelessness depicted in this photograph of a women's ward at Willard from the early 1960s.

The use of neuroleptic drugs did not slow the use of electroshock, possibly because the latter was still the cheaper method. Former Willard occupational therapist Nancy Jaycot Caniff recalls an almost assembly-line-like procedure from the early 1960s:

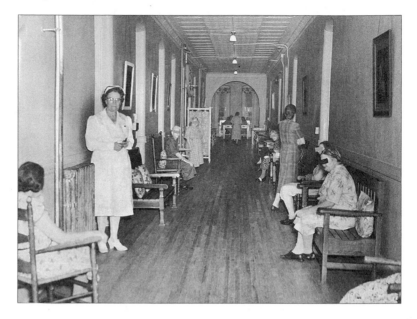

NC: *I started working there back when they used to line up for shock treat-ments and. . . . They had what they called the blitz, and you'd go in and you had your shock treatment. That's when people broke their backs and everything when they had shock because they weren't sedated or anything. And they'd line up the chairs in the hallway and there'd probably be fifteen or twenty people. And they'd take this one in and give her shock and then she'd go to the end of the line and they would blitz them two or three times that day . . .*

DP: *And people didn't try to avoid shock treatment? They just accepted it?*

NC: *Oh, no. Some people were petrified of shock treatment. It was a real scary thing. It was scary to watch. You had people holding you down, trying to hold you down because the neck would arch up and they had this big thing they put in their mouth. Now, if you have shock treat-ments, they give you a sedative. Back then, they didn't. They gave them nothing. Back then they convulsed terrible. It was real scary to see. And it was kind of scary to even walk through the wards, you know. People were put into their little rooms naked.*

Throughout the 1930s and 1940s, electroshock dominated the treat-ment at places like Willard, spreading fear, intimidation, and a certain degree of confusion among the inmates. When drugs were added to the treatment regimen during the 1950s, it must have seemed as if a huge cot-ton-filled blanket had settled over those wards, muffling the sounds and leaving the patients shuffling along like mindless automatons.

APPALLING CONDITIONS, CORRECTIVE ACTIONS

After World War II, several exposés of appalling conditions in state hospitals brought public scrutiny to the field; these included a photo essay in *Life* magazine by Albert Maisel in 1946 and a 1948 book by journalist Albert Deutsch, entitled *The Shame of the States*. Maisel described and photographed patients in deplorable conditions, such as people strapped into chairs on wards infested with rats; he described these people as "guiltless patient-prisoners." These exposés prompted investigative committees at both state and national levels that recommended downsizing the state hospital systems and providing more treatment in the community, but progress toward this goal was slow.

In the 1960s, Willard began to offer new services aimed at releasing long-stay patients like the suitcase owners. By then most of them were elderly, and after decades locked away, they were in no condition to return to their communities as independent citizens. Instead, the hospital staff tried to get them ready for transfer to a foster home ("family care"), board and care facilities, or nursing homes. Ironically, some of those places were the very same poorhouses that had sent patients to Willard in the nineteenth century. But even such seemingly modest goals took a great deal of effort. After decades at Willard, most patients had become so habituated to hospital life that they could not envision learning the skills required to live in a world that had changed drastically since they last lived freely in it.

HOW DID PEOPLE RESPOND
TO HOSPITALIZATION?

The suitcase owners' responses to decades of hospitalization ranged from resignation to resistance, from despair to the hope that they might someday be released. In the medical records, one finds no indication that any of them thought their confinement at Willard was warranted or that they benefited from being there. Some seemed resigned to their fate and others tried to make the best of their situations. At one extreme, people like Margaret, Herman, Irma, Frank, and Theresa simply shut down, retreating into an inner world of their own. Others did what they could to occupy their time and make the best of an unfortunate situation. Ethel kept active by knitting, socializing, and helping around the ward. Rodrigo busied himself with reading, writing poetry, and, in his old age, helping his fellow patients. Dmytre and Lawrence were able to find some meaning in their lives; the former through his painting and the latter in his role as the hospital's grave digger. Madeline alone was consistently defiant; she never lost her belief that her incarceration was a serious injustice, insisted for decades that she didn't belong there and could return to work, and demanded her release at every opportunity.

But even those people who seemed acquiescent occasionally showed flashes of resistance to their fate. Dmytre pleaded to return home to continue building his house in Syracuse and made several escape attempts. Lawrence wrote to the superintendent demanding his freedom and back pay for his work. Even Margaret, who seemed passive and grimly resigned, occasionally asked to be allowed to go home. Rodrigo, who was seen by the staff as a model patient, clearly understood his hospitalization as a curtailment of his liberty; early in his patienthood, he wrote to his uncle, "I have no definite knowledge yet of when I shall regain my freedom."

8.
A PHOTOGRAPHIC
TALENT:
RISING ABOVE
THE FRAY

The body of Herman Graham is buried in a family plot at the Mount Olivet Cemetery in Maspeth, New York, not far from where he was born. His name is not listed among his relatives on the tombstone. He finally rejoined the fold, anonymously. He only made a few trips home during his forty-five years away, one of them listed as an elopement from the Craig Colony for Epileptics in Sonyea (State of New York Epileptic Association), New York, where his parents sent him to treat the seizures that came on after an early childhood bout of meningitis. Craig Colony was the first U.S. institution of its kind, modeled after the pioneering Bethel Epilepsy Center in Bielefeld, Germany. The notion that people suffering from seizures could be helped by a long stay in a specialized institution seems misguided today, since ever more effective anti-epileptic drugs have been developed. Back in the 1920s, going to the Colony was banishment and hope at once. Removing epileptics from the dangers of community life, and thereby limiting public exposure to disturbing attacks, meant hitting two birds with one stone. Remarkably, Graham was among those Colonists who may have benefited the most from being shipped several hundred miles away from home.

EPILEPSY BIOGRAPHS

As a patient, Herman Graham assisted the pathologist at the Craig Colony, Dr. Henry Munson, in making photographic records of post-mortem examinations. At that time, around 1913, fresh brains of subjects with a variety of neurological conditions were a prized commodity. The doctors there went so far as to petition the New York State legislature for permission to perform autopsies without the patients' or their families' consent. The legislators did not object, and so everyone who died there came under the knife. Colony doctors were also among the first to make use of photography and film in documenting their observations of the patients in their charge.

In 1909, in the first-ever undertaking of its kind, Boston neurologist Dr. Walter Chase brought a film crew to Sonyea and lined up more than one hundred patients in their beds outside the dorms, under the sun, waiting for someone to seize. When that happened, the giant camera was quickly lugged next to the person's bedside and the seizure recorded. These "Epilepsy Biographs" were the first visual records of sudden and erratic movements, a pioneering feat of motion photography. This apparently started a brief but remarkable period of cinematic and photographic recordings at the Craig Colony, and Herman played an important role. When he arrived at Sonyea, the earliest films were being shot, and he would likely have noticed the buzz this generated. Many patients were filmed in the midst of seizures or other abnormal movements. These rare films are now among the cherished of early cinematic accomplishments, even though they added little to the advancement of epilepsy research. If anything, they are rather degrading and difficult to watch, lacking the pretense of scientific inquiry.

Actual brain dissections, on the other hand, permitted the recording of obvious malformations that may have been connected to aberrant behavior or neurological symptoms. Graham trained his camera and lenses that were stored for over fifty years in the Willard attic, on the mortal remains of his fellow Colonists. He was undoubtedly among the Colony's elite, with

his coveted job, no obvious disabilities, and only rare seizures. Visiting the former Colony today, which has been converted into a medium security prison, one can still tour the original cottages on the Village Green where "higher class" patients like Graham enjoyed their considerable liberties.

He was not entirely pleased to be packed up and shipped away from his home turf in Maspeth at the age of twenty-two. He had already suffered an operation on his skull as a young boy to relieve pressure on the brain caused by purulent meningitis, the only hope for relief in the era before antibiotics. The surgery left Herman with mild paralysis on his left side, which did not prevent him from taking up metal lathing at the age of fourteen. He also worked for some time in a glue factory, but quit this job around the age of seventeen when he began to have grand mal seizures that were surely frightening to co-workers and put the boy in harm's way. Apparently, Herman's seizures were preceded by a physical warning that started on his left side and generalized to the rest of his body, rendering him unconscious and putting him to sleep for a while afterward. With the seizures becoming more frequent and intractable, his family went looking for a remedy outside of their community. Craig Colony had opened a few years before Herman had his first seizure, and it rapidly became the state-of-the-art in managing epilepsy.

As William P. Spratling, M.D., the medical superintendent, explained in the Twelfth Annual Report to the Board of Managers of the Craig Colony for Epileptics, on October 1, 1905:

> Many epileptics who cannot be completely cured may be made to enjoy long immunity from attacks by adhering strictly to a proper mode of living; so that freedom from epilepsy is often merely a matter of right living. Scores of epileptics now at the Colony who seldom have attacks cannot live anywhere else in the same way. Some go a year or longer without a seizure and think they are cured only to be disillusioned when they quit the Colony and the wholesome ways of living they had to observe while here.

But Herman was homesick and took off for New York City, to the embarrassment of his family, who promptly sent the boy back upstate. This took some political pull, as the facility was overwhelmed with requests for admission, since it was the only place of its kind in the entire state. Maybe they kept a better eye on him in subsequent years, or maybe Herman got used to institutional life with its various trappings—many Colonists wore fancy uniforms and generally acted like members of a gentlemen's club—but this time he stayed. There was a distinct hierarchy among residents, between those who had obvious disabilities and were generally considered feebleminded, and those who seemed perfectly fine during their interictal episodes—the time free of seizures—which for those who took to the "treatment" became ever more extended. Herman was among those whose seizures became less and less frequent. Doctors reckoned that he had three seizures a month during the two years prior to his admission. After his initial adjustment period, he experienced only four seizures in the twenty-three years he spent at the Colony, at a sizable cost to the state. It is likely that some families of means paid for the care of their relatives at the Colony, but in Herman's case, we have no record of such payments. His father died young and his mother took care of Herman's four siblings on her own. They were undoubtedly not among the wealthier folks of Maspeth, New York.

By the time Graham started to work in the morgue, he had been seizure-free for several years, undoubtedly a requirement for being trusted with such a sensitive assignment. Herman was more interested in photography than in neuropathology, and he looked upon his work as an opportunity to learn more about the art of taking pictures, which was becoming a rather lucrative do-it-yourself type of occupation. Mail-order courses were available and Herman's belongings show us how he first learned about such opportunities and signed up for a course. It is uncertain where he obtained funds for the equipment he bought and the tuition fee for the school he joined, but he quickly became an eager student.

The path from morgue assistant to portrait photographer with his own studio on the green of Craig Colony was unusual for someone who would have been shunned by society, had his seizures not come under some degree of control. Undoubtedly, other Colonists were involved in all types of work, as most state institutions relied on patient labor to whatever extent possible. In most cases, such labor was exploited for the benefit of the facility and its residents, not for the personal business interest of one man. At Willard, patients did much of the menial work, and also some specialized jobs such as shoemaking and tailoring, which were necessary for running the place. This was equally true at Craig Colony. But few patients would have had the opportunity to come into personal wealth as a result of a business enterprise operating on state grounds. Paper routes, maybe growing some vegetables, or owning a shoe-shine box were possible exceptions. In 1915, Herman acquired a professional camera, a set of excellent lenses, and all the darkroom equipment needed to provide his customers with professional prints. Staff and Colonists apparently enjoyed the opportunity to have their portraits taken and paid him accordingly. Herman took pictures of his fellow residents, introducing a different aesthetic than the one favored by the medical staff.

Today, a great deal of importance is placed on the value of supportive peer-to-peer relationships among individuals with disabilities in general, and people with psychiatric problems in particular. In Graham's case, it was probably not so much an identification with his subjects that allowed him

Craig Colony, c. 1927

to portray them in their fullest humanity, posing in a relaxed fashion, looking straight at the camera, without any apparent deformities or unusual movements. It might have been the choice of individuals—unlike the film footage shot at the institution in those years, which concentrated on unusual types—but it was also the photographer's eye, which was eager to portray his subjects in the most favorable manner. Like his more famous predecessor, Dr. Hugh Diamond, who traded his profession psychiatry for the art of portrait photography, Herman took care to avoid a focus on pathology, and instead emphasized the dignity, humanity, and companionship of his willing subjects.

For many years, the Colony administrators allowed Herman to go about his business with little fanfare or concern. In fact, they appeared to be somewhat in awe of his ability to set up a business, solicit customers, and keep himself financially afloat for some time.

MARCH 30, 1918: *He is quite ambitious and has purchased on the installment plan, a fine lens. His work has increased and earns fifteen or twenty dollars a month. Had a superior attitude towards other patients because of his achievements in photography.*

But when the creditors came knocking, the doctors' sentiments turned from benign ignorance to sordid confrontation:

APRIL 1, 1922: *Has no idea of paying his just debts. Recently he secured a stereopticon light from the relative of a patient. It was with considerable difficulty that the latter secured the money. He still owes Mark and Fuller something over $180.00 for photographic supplies bought in past years.*

From these entries, we can see that Herman had fallen behind on his payments to his photographic suppliers, either because he couldn't or didn't care to make good on his commitments. We know almost nothing about the way he was thinking, how he was conducting his business, and to what extent he was staying on top of his books. One thing is clear: he did not ask for help from Colony staff, nor was such help offered, at least according to the information in the record; all he got was an embarrassing confrontation in the superintendent's office.

Today, the idea that someone with a mental or physical disability would be able to start their own small business does not seem unusual. Why should a person with an entrepreneurial spirit who finds himself in the mental health system not be encouraged to pursue his business ideas? The federal Small Business Administration and many state vocational rehabilitation agencies support individual business plans, although the rate of success is admittedly low.

Graham did not have access to those kinds of resources. As a self-starter, he might have had a hard time asking for support once he needed it. Pride and shame may have made it hard to admit that he was falling on bad times and could not figure out how to keep up with his debt. And the doctors certainly did not make it any easier for him. When he was on top of his game, his photos adorned many an employee's mantelpiece and appeared in the Colony's annual reports.

When he fell on hard times, the staff treated him like the patient that he was, pulling rank and reminding him of his duties. "Reality therapy," some might call it, but the doctors' intervention appeared to have a less than therapeutic effect.

When Herman was admitted to Craig Colony for the second time in 1908, he was just twenty-three years old and had lost his father not too long before. After he absconded from the Colony earlier that year, he was taken to the Farm Colony on Staten Island for a short stint before being brought back to Sonyea, three hundred miles from home. The Farm Colony was an unusual place, but it was not specially designated for epileptics:

> While the inmates at other institutions under the Department of Public Charities look around and have nothing whatever to do, here they pay for their board twofold by their labor, working on the farm raising vegetables, not only for themselves, but for other unfortunates. No healthier spot within miles of Greater New York can be found, situated on the western slope of Todt Hill, the highest land in Greater New York—it being 368 feet above sea level—a beautiful site with its fertile fields, where any kind of vegetable thrives. All it needs is cultivation . . .

When he arrived at Craig Colony, his physical exam found him a "well-nourished male" five feet three and a half inches tall and weighing 120 pounds, a rather slender and diminutive young man, nothing like the stocky person he became after years of institutional food. The doctor found his "frontal region rather narrow and his hairline low. Very slight drooping of upper eyelids but no ptosis . . . some paralysis of the left hand and forearm, some very slight wasting in the fingers of his left arm." These are relatively minor neurological impairments, the result of meningitis and the surgery he received. His first seizure was said to have occurred between age sixteen and seventeen, more than ten years after being "trephined on the right side of his vertex"; in other words, after he had a hole drilled into the right side of his skull.

Notes were written in the Craig Colony "Abstract of History," which was included in his Willard chart, at yearly or six-month intervals. In 1910, he worked daily; in 1911, he was "inclined to be over-bearing toward fellow patients and sometimes abuses smaller boys"—signs of a bully or a successful businessman? He had only one seizure that year and no more until 1919. His photography work began in 1914, when his chart says he aided "in the developing room in the Laboratory"—a euphemism for the morgue. By mid-1915, he began his own photography work on the side and was "well behaved and on the whole a model patient." His business took off in 1918; he was said to exhibit "considerable egotism" and was "quite ambitious." It was also reported that he had "a superior attitude toward other patients because of his achievements in photography." On March 20, 1919, Herman suffered his first grand mal seizure in more than six years; it was said that he had been worrying over his finances for some time. A year later he bounced back, even went on a ten-day vacation to New York City, but more financial troubles lay ahead. By 1922, he was said to owe $180 to Mark & Fuller for photographic supplies. He had two mild attacks in 1922, and one seizure recorded in 1923.

A mysterious change began in 1924. First he "flew into a rage" when confronted with his outstanding debt and supposedly denied all responsibility. Then he started to have migraines and the doctors surmised that these were "replacing" the seizures. Despite the fact that he began another correspondence course on photography in 1926, he was described as indifferent to his work, often stayed in bed all day, didn't honor his commitments to customers, and his business fell off. August 23, 1928: "Gets orders from patients for pictures, never takes them, or after taking and developing he never finishes them."

Less than three months later, he had a bout of suspiciousness, fearing that his food was poisoned, and refused to eat or drink. After a few days in a hospital, "he finally clear[ed]." But in January 1929, he was "found in bed masturbating!" By July, the doctors deemed his mental condition greatly impaired and dull; they reported that he was unable to "retain any question for any time. Refuses to work. Wanders off the Colony very frequently."

Undoubtedly something had changed for the worse after he was confronted with his debt. Could he have taken this so deeply to heart that he drifted into a melancholic state? Did he realize that no matter how hard he worked, he could never meet his obligations, and that his business was doomed? Many people, primarily men, fell into despair during the Great Depression, but Graham's collapse preceded the stock market crash by a few years. His decline was gradual but was apparently prompted by economic woes.

The last entry in his Craig Colony record is dated October 1, 1930, and mentions that he had no seizures that year, and was "sullen and morose," but in good physical condition. Only two weeks earlier, he received a Tuition Certificate confirming that he had paid $96 to the American School of Photography in Chicago for a Course in Modern Photography, which included a free view camera as a bonus. This camera probably did not arrive at the Colony before Herman left; it was not the one that ended up in his trunk. We do not know how he came up with the $96 in the face of his financial obligations, but we can be certain that the doctors' notes do not tell the whole story. Herman had not given up on himself while his doctors were already scheming about pawning off their unruly patient, who dodged his debtors and customers and was caught masturbating in bed, to the mental health system. About a month later, Herman stood before psychiatrist Dr. J. Moses, who conducted his admission interview at Willard.

FROM THE MENTAL EXAMINATION OF OCTOBER 30, 1930:

DR. MOSES: How old were you when you had your first convulsion?

H. GRAHAM: 16 or 17.

DR.:   While you were working?

HG: I was sick for three months and I quit work.

DR.:   What was the matter?

HG: My stomach.

DR.:   Did you have meningitis?

HG: Not that I know of.

DR.:   Did you have a doctor?

HG: Yes.

DR.:   After you got up you had your first attack of epilepsy?

HG: Yes.

DR.:   How often did you have them?

HG: They left me for 6 to 8 years.

DR.:   How many would you have?

HG: Two a year one every six months.

DR.:   Did they bother you much?

HG: No.

DR.:   Did you know when you were going to have one?

HG: Yes.

DR.: How?

HG: Tingling in my left arm.

DR.: How old were you when you went to Craig Colony?

HG: 20.

DR.: You ran away from there, didn't you?

HG: Once, but I went back again.

DR.: Did you have a lot of seizures while you were up there?

HG: Three or four attacks.

DR.: What did you do?

HG: Photography.

DR.: Make a lot of money?

HG: $30.00 a day sometimes.

DR.: Who did you work for?

HG: Dr. Munson.

DR.: You use to photograph patients?

HG: Yes.

DR.: How did you make $30.00 a day that way?

HG: I used to work for myself.

DR.: Did you get along good at Sonyea?

HG: Yes.

. . .

DR.: You know what kind of hospital this is, don't you?

HG: Insane.

DR.: Are you insane?

HG: That is up to you.

DR.: What do you think about it?

HG: I don't know anything about it. There are violent people here.

DR.: Why do you think they sent you here?

HG: I don't know.

DR.: Do you think you are crazy?

HG: No.

DR.: Did you complain that the food was poison?

HG: Not that I know of.

DR.: Think anyone was plotting against you?

HG: No. A fellow having a couple of spells would go this way.

DR.: You think following a couple of spells you said these things?

HG: Yes.

DR.: Did they ever tell you you said these things?

HG: No.

DR.: Did you used to get violent following these seizures?

HG: No. I haven't had one in two years.

DR.: They said you refused to pay for your lens and things.

HG: They are all paid for.

DR.: Are you worth any money?

HG: Not now.

DR.: Who do you blame for your being here?

HG: No one. I might have took sick and got a little delirious and did not know what I was doing.

DR.: How do you feel about the whole business now?

HG: Good.

DR.: Like it here?

HG: Not a bad place. About the same as Craig Colony.

DR.: Are you satisfied with the treatment here?

HG: Yes it is alright.

DR.: Do you think if we put you out in one of our outside buildings you would like it better?

HG: It is alright.

DR.: Would you like to work in one of our dining rooms?

HG: I couldn't do that work.

DR.: Are you satisfied with being here?

HG: You have to be.

DR.: Worried about anything?

HG: Not just now.

DR.: What do you think about the whole business?

HG: I couldn't tell you.

DR.: You think you are alright?

HG: Yes.

DR.: Good as you ever was?

HG: Yes.

At the end of his five-page evaluation, Dr. Moses made the following entry: "At times during the examination it appeared quite evident that this patient was not suffering from any psychosis of any kind and the examiner could see no reason for this patient being at a state institution for the insane."

Why did the first institution offer him so many chances, while the second one condemned him to decades of idleness until he died? Was this a function of different treatment philosophies, or was it merely the result of a man's melancholia for which no treatment was available yet?

When he entered Willard, Herman's camera and lenses were stowed away in the attic, never to be used again. For the next thirty-five years, he did no photographic work but helped with light office duties. He did not understand why he was being kept at Willard, but felt he did not have anywhere else to go.

Here are some of the things his doctors had to say about him over his thirty-five years of his stay at Willard:

Dr. H. B. Luidens (1930–1936): "cooperative and tries to do some work."

Dr. A. R. Gildea (1937–1938): "cooperative, obeys orders, but does not do much work except polishing."

Dr. Laughlin (1944): "says he feels contented here."

Dr. Guthiel (1948 and 1951): "helped with the office and other light duties."

Dr. Jackamets (1951): "clean and neat in his appearance."

Dr. Waxman (1955): "mingles well with other patients."

Dr. Kadri Gungor (1960-1962): "cooperative, coherent, and relevant."

Dr. H. F. Weinauer (1962-1965): "sociable and shows interest in his surroundings."

Dr. A. Jansons (November 25, 1965): "Patient was . . . placed on critical November 25, 1965, because of Arteriosclerotic Heart Disease and congestion of the lungs. He went downhill rapidly and expired on November 25, 1965."

Dr. George J. Buchholtz, Assistant Clinical Director (November 25, 1965): "DISCHARGED The note written by Dr. Jansons concerning patient's death was reviewed. The patient is today removed from the hospital records by virtue of death."

On November 26, 1965, Herman's sister Anna wrote the following to Dr. Anthony Mustille, the director of the hospital:

Dear Sir, Go ahead on a post-mortem on Herman G. Thank you for taking care of him these long years.

The postmortem was never performed.

9.
A FREQUENT VISITOR
TO THE
WHITE HOUSE

Dmytre Zarchuk died on January 21, 2001, at the age of eighty-four, six years after his suitcase was found. He lived in rural Chemong County at a private home for psychiatric patients whose dining room is still cheered up by a mural Dmytre had painted there. It shows the three buildings of this former poorhouse on a snowy lawn with yellow, green, and blue stars. Mr. Zarchuk was much loved there, as he sat in his chair and scribbled Cyrillic notes in a diary, now lost. He spent nearly two-thirds of his life in American mental institutions.

Dmytre and his new wife, Sofia, arrived in the United States after World War II on a favored Displaced Persons status. A carpenter and a nurse, they were welcome in the postwar economy by the Ukrainian exile community of Syracuse, New York. Decent work and a loan to build a house were quickly obtained. But it took just one cataclysmic event to turn Mr. Zarchuk's life from the beginning prosperity of a new immigrant into the unremitting drudgery of a chronic mental patient. And it took the attention of one occupational therapist at the state hospital to reawaken his creative powers after seven years in a despondent state.

BELONGINGS

Dmytre Zarchuk's suitcase contained 199 items, all neatly bagged and cataloged by curators. Among them were: 14 paper patterns for wooden cutouts of various animals, a glider plane, crèche figures, and a small doll's carriage; a colored print of Madonna and Child from Innsbruck, Tyrol; a paisley scarf and three peach-colored towels; a hand-sewn white cotton ladies' outfit: blouse, skirt, jacket, and belt with five embroidered stars; two bedsheets, an alarm clock and a hand-carved wooden dog; a bronze model of the Washington Monument; and pamphlets, dictionaries, and religious booklets in German, Ukrainian, and English.

> 32643.26 PHOTO ALBUM, *13 pages with 39 black and white photographs, some have writing on back, some are loose, two have been hand colored. One photograph appears to be Sofia Jaromij and Dmytre Z's wedding. The dress she is wearing is in this collection as are the artificial flowers in her bouquet and a ribbon from boutonniere.*

Also in the suitcase was a metal container with lid and four aluminum shot glasses inside; a sewing kit, gift of the American Red Cross; a blood donor pin; silver fork and spoon with ornate flower pattern; seven notebooks with calculations; twenty-six postcards (Salzburg Mirabell-Gardens, Franciscan Preparatory Seminary, Hollidaysburg, Pennsylvania; Enns,

Upper Danube; St. Thomas More, House of Studies, Washington, D.C.; Chapel Window, Hospital of the Good Shepherd, Syracuse, New York; *Maid of the Mist*, Niagara Falls; Union Station, Lincoln Memorial, Library of Congress, Washington Monument, Washington, D.C.).

Patients were permitted few personal items on the wards. Some had a nightstand with a drawer. Two or three sets of clothing were stored in a communal closet. Those who worked in other buildings or on the sprawling grounds might have had work clothes, boots, and rain gear. Whoever was confined to the ward had less; nothing was allowed that might cause harm to self or others, like belts, hammers, hairpins, or bottle openers. Dmytre left the facility in 1977 without his wedding pictures, his immigration papers, and the many mementos of his life.

ARTISTRY

Dmytre Zarchuk was a natural artisan. At Willard he became an artist. He made gouache paintings and brightly colored murals in the folk art manner of his native country. One of his paintings was shown in a 1966 exhibit of "patient art" at the American Psychiatric Association in Washington, D.C. A masterwork was found in the office of a former Willard employee, who had been transferred to another facility when the hospital closed. It is a portrait of his hometown, Utoropy.

"Utoropy Village," by Dmytre Zarchuk, c. 1960

D.Z. continues to be a lone worker. He paints in watercolors and does copies and original compositions. Patient seems to be a little more aware of other people and somewhat more receptive of suggestions. Upon sale of two of his pictures for $2.00, patient bought a selection of candy and distributed it to all other patients and employees in the ward day-room. . . . Patient is sometimes observed laughing heartily to himself.

Art therapy and artistic creation by mental patients often serve opposing ends. When a patient produces art for analysis and therapeutic benefit, authorship is considered irrelevant. When a patient creates works for his or her own purposes, they are rarely accepted as the authentic renderings of observations, fantasies, and inner experiences. On occasion, such works have seized the attention of doctors who sponsor and collect patient art. Van Gogh had his Dr. Gachet; the Swiss genius draughtsman Kurt Woelfli, his Dr. Morgenthaler, and the recently rediscovered Martin Ramirez, his psychologist Dr. Tarmo Pasto, who organized his first gallery show. Scores of patients in mental institutions had psychiatrists peering over their shoulders as they created drawings, woodcuts, oils, sculptures, and installations. With the recent craving for "outsider art," many works by patients are flowing into the art market, bringing small bits of fame to their creators, often belatedly, and considerable profits to their exhibitors.

"Each painting he did depicted a part of his life," said Nancy Jaycot Caniff in 2003. "And it started out with this village in the Ukraine and went on to when he was in the concentration camps [sic] and then coming over here on a boat. Oh, there must be probably fifty really good pictures someplace. There must be that many. Most of them were of his life."

To understand Dmytre's painting of his ancestral home, it is important to know that in 1899 a fire destroyed Utoropy's fabulous Greek-Catholic church, which was rebuilt in Dmytre's birth year on a hill overlooking the town. His painting places the church back in its original location, at the center of the village round. Utoropy has a rich history. It is one of the oldest Hutsul villages and celebrated its 630th anniversary in 1998. It is also the "first Ukrainian village on the Internet."* The Hutsuls settled on the northern slopes of the Carpathian Mountains between the fourteenth and eighteenth centuries. They are distinct from the surrounding Slavic peoples in physiognomy and in their traditional culture of Romanian and Balkan origin, apparent in their clothing, customs, cuisine, architecture, and faith. At one point, Dmytre's brother Jurko sent a handwoven Hutsul carpet as a gift to the superintendent of Willard—a vivid illustration of Dmytre's cultural background.

---

* At *http://members.tripod.com /utoropy/index_e.htm.*

EAST OR WEST

The 23-year old Dmytre was arrested in Utoropy by the German invaders in the winter of 1939 and sent to an Austrian farm as a slave laborer. He never made his way back home after the war.

In a letter to President Harry Truman, Dmytre wrote many years later:

I came to the farmer and tell to the farmer that I want to swim the River Enns. I want to come to American Zone. At night I live close by the farmer. The farmer give me a rubber from a car wheel and I swam the river. I came good through the river. I overnight by the farmer. Then I find wife for me and stay there this was Kronstorf there I was a few months.

Kronstorf had been taken by the 635th Tank Destroyer Battalion of the Kansas National Guard on May 6, 1945. This small town became a magnet for people trying to cross into the American sector. Sofia Jaromij was a Polish refugee who fled westward, like Dmytre, when the Russians advanced. They went to a Displaced Person camp near Salzburg, where they were married, trained

"As a memento, on July 26, 1944, from your employer, Stöckler, Franz"

From wedding album, Dmytre Z. and Sofia J., c. 1946

in their respective professions, and finally, after three years, obtained the visa they were waiting for.

On December 5, 1951, three years after their arrival in the United States, Sofia entered St. Joseph's Hospital, where she was employed as a nurse, with a miscarriage in progress. A few hours later, she was dead from bleeding that could not be stopped.

D.C. BOUND

Dmytre was bereft, and yet, for a while, he continued to do what was expected. He received condolences from friends, kept working, took English classes and kept building the house on a hill overlooking the Ukrainian graveyard where Sofia was laid to rest. In 1952, he traveled to Washington and went to the White House trying to see the president. He stayed at the YMCA and patronized the Library of Congress.

Soon after arriving in America, Dmytre had built a scale replica of the wooden church in his hometown as a gift of gratitude to President Truman. He delivered it by hand to the White House mailroom and received the following letter of acknowledgment in July 1950.

> *Through the courtesy of the White House this Commission is in the possession of a replica of an ancient church of your home town . . . in Western Ukraine. The Commission is grateful for the opportunity to exhibit the gift of your model—complete with altar, lights, stained glass windows and bells—of the church, a bell tower and a caretaker's house. This manifestation of your work—the patience required to complete such a splendid model—shall be an inspiration both to the personnel of the Displaced Persons Commission as well as to anyone having the privilege of viewing it. Please accept the thanks of this commission and it is our earnest hope that you are very happy in your new home, the United States of America.*

Two years later, on September 30, 1952, Dmytre Zarchuk was apprehended by the Secret Service outside the White House, trying to make contact with Margaret Truman, the president's daughter. That same day, he was admitted to Gallinger Municipal Hospital in Washington, D.C., for "mental observation." Two weeks later, he was found to be of unsound mind in the U.S. District Court for the District of Columbia and was transferred to St. Elizabeth's Hospital.

MENTAL STATUS ON ADMISSION:
He was friendly and pleasant and [his] answers were in general coherent, though he had difficulty in explaining his situation and was confused as to happenings preceding his admission to Gallinger. He continued to express delusions concerning his identification with Christ and his relation to the

President's daughter. He denied hallucinatory experiences. He showed no insight into his mental illness. . . .

DIAGNOSIS: *SCHIZOPHRENIC REACTION. ACUTE UNDIFFERENTIATED TYPE.*

CONDITION ON DISCHARGE: *UNIMPROVED.*

On April 25, 1953, Dmytre was sent on to Syracuse Psychopathic Hospital.

FIRST ADMISSION: *The patient was pleasant, cooperative, alert but withdrawn. In discussions not related to Margaret Truman he was coherent. Emotionally he was cheerful. He spoke with resignation about his personal tragedy. There was no change in his delusional trend and he showed complete lack of insight and inappropriate judgment. He was diagnosed as DEMENTIA PRAECOX, PARANOID TYPE.*

Three weeks later he arrived at Willard State Hospital.

<u>Mentally</u> *the patient was clean, neat, quiet, idle, disinterested in ward activities. His speech was coherent giving evidence of his various fixed delusional ideas. Emotionally he showed regression being seclusive, withdrawn, and suspicious. Occasionally he became irritable and showing some paranoid attitude. His sensorium is relatively intact. There was inappropriate judgment and complete lack of insight.*

A little more than a month after his admission, he was moved to the North Wing, designated for patients deemed incurable. Within days, he was given his first course of electroshock.

AUGUST 20, 1953:
Patient has improved considerably. He is clean and neat in appearance, is somewhat restless and agitated, and during the entire interview he is quite talkative and circumstantial. He denies his delusional ideas as previously expressed and claims that he was misunderstood by the physician on his previous hospitalization. He is still somewhat suspicious and evasive. He is oriented and shows some memory deficits. He is today TRANSFERRED from Ward 2 to Ward 9 in order to give him an opportunity to adjust on a quieter ward.

Less than a week after the electroshock, he wrote a letter to the president, which was never mailed, asking for his release.

Six weeks later, from a doctor's note in his medical chart:

Willard state <u>I</u>
25. August 1953.
Dear Mr. Harry Truman.
Truman. Margareta Truman.
Zacharuk when come from
ton D. C. to Syracuse N. y. Den
atton. Mie lucet in
bunge mie

OCTOBER 2, 1953:   ESCAPE ATTEMPT

Patient continues to be clean and tidy in his habits and appearance, quiet and cooperative. He has been working recently in the main kitchen and was able to get along quite well with other patients and employees. There are no hallucinations or delusions at present, but he is still very evasive, argumentative, demanding, and has absolutely no insight or judgment. This morning at about 9 o'clock, patient ran away. He was found walking on the main hospital street. . . . He was brought back to the North Wing and was immediately interviewed by the writer. He was slightly confused, definitely restless, and occasionally irrelevant. The only explanation he could give was that he does not belong to the hospital anymore and he just wanted to go to Syracuse to see his home . . .

SEPTEMBER 29, 1954: *Representatives of the United States Department of Justice this date interviewed this patient relative to his status as a deportable alien.*

FEBRUARY 10, 1955: *This 38 year old, white, short and well nourished patient has been interviewed today in order to fill in the deportation papers. It was very difficult to get the proper information because patient is very paranoid, suspicious, incoherent, and irrelevant. Some questions had to be repeated many times until the patient gave the answer. Instead of giving a direct answer, he would talk about his persecutory ideas and at times it was quite impossible to interrupt his worthless productions. He claims that somebody murdered his wife and he would not sign the papers for deportation until the Government finds out who the murderers are and punishes them. After two hours of interview, the papers were filled out and signed by the patient. However, the value of the statements must be considered as questionable. . . .*   —Dr. B. Huk/mvn-9NW

DISPLACED PERSON

From a handwritten letter by Dmytre dated March 25, 1957, addressed to the American Red Cross:

*House built by Dmytre Z.,
301 Salisbury Road, Syracuse.*

I came 1948 to U.S.A. to Syracuse N.Y. to work. 1952 Syracuse N.Y. arrested me for nothing for Jesus Christ that I am Jesus Christ. And after bring me to Willard State Hospital Jail. And this Hospital will not live [sic] me from here. Three times I was going back to Syracuse N.Y. to work and they bring me back and will not tell what they want from me. I please very much American Red Cross that American Red Cross help me that the Hospital live [sic] me from here. That I can go back to Syracuse N.Y. On Salisbury Road 301 I have my own House that I have place where to life [sic]. When American Red Cross can not help me that I can go back to Syracuse N.Y. to work then I please very much that American Red Cross help me that I can go to Europe to Bremerhaven.

For years after his walk away from the hospital, it was felt that "the patient is still looking for an occasion to escape from the hospital," since he believed that he was being detained without justification, and had threatened a court procedure. He was housed on a locked unit, but still permitted to attend occupational therapy (OT).

The chart entry dated September 3, 1957, said:

Patient's letter addressed to "People in Elliott Hall" is attached to the record as a sample of patients delusions. In this letter, he claims to be innocent and kept against his wish in the hospital just because he is Jesus Christ. Of course, this is only one of his delusions but characteristic enough for his present mental condition. —Dr. B. Huk/mvn-3NW

DEMENTIA PRAECOX

The first diagnosis Dmytre received was "schizophrenic reaction," a concept introduced in 1920 by E. Popper for "single schizophrenic manifestations of short duration and full recovery, occurring after a traumatic experience." The notion that psychotic symptoms like delusions could be reactions to traumatic events and therefore understandable has been around since at least 1913, when Karl Jaspers published his seminal work *General Psychopathology*. The psychiatrists at Willard obviously did not subscribe to this theory, as they carefully separated Dmytre's reaction to Sofia's death from his "paranoid delusions."

The fact that his doctors dismissed a connection between his mental state and his experiences prior to his White House caper might have sealed his fate as a chronic mental patient. His notion of returning to Syracuse to get his job and house back was certainly considered irrational. Dmytre's attempts to find an explanation for the unfathomable or simply to pick up where he left off found no sympathetic ear among the hospital staff.

From a handwritten letter by Dmytre dated January 31, 1958:

Proud of Jesus Christ!
Dear Policeman Syracuse N.Y. . . . Syracuse N.Y. arrested me for nothing for that that [sic] I am Jesus Christ. . . . In 1951 my wife was working and fell down, the boss there [at] work tell to my wife . . . [to go to the] hospital. My wife [went] . . . to St. Joseph's Hospital. There some bandits come to my wife and tell [her that she can not] come out from there, [that she] just must make [an] operation. . . . Then make operation. My wife died. I came to the hospital and ask what [happened to] my wife Sofia? . . . Some bandits killed my wife in the middle of the night. . . . The operation was not so bad [it] was on the side of her back. [One year after my wife died, in 1952] some bandits go to kill me for that that [sic] I am Jesus Christ and do not have an excuse [to] live. My wife [was killed] by some bandits for that that [sic] was Jesus Christ. . . . I please very much Policeman Syracuse N.Y. . . . maybe you can find who killed my wife. . . . If you cannot help [me to] go back to Syracuse N.Y. you help me that I can go back to Europe . . .

At Willard, seven months after his arrest, Dr. Herbert Goldsman gave Dmytre a new diagnosis: Dementia praecox, paranoid type. Goldsman had been trained when this term was still widely used. By 1953 the Willard psychiatrists had not made the transition from dementia praecox to schizophrenia even though the term *schizophrenia* had been used over fifteen hundred times in the psychiatric literature during the preceding ten years, whereas dementia praecox appeared less than a hundred times. Willard's lack of "progress" in this area suggests a persistent belief that their patients were bound to deteriorate rather than recover.

Technically, in 1953, Dmytre Zarchuk was still in the midst of his first psychotic episode, which certainly would have merited more active treatment, even according to the pessimistic views of the time.

A SHOCKING TREATMENT

Upon admission to his "chronic" service, Dr. Goldsman noted that Dmytre was:

clean and neat in his appearance and tidy in his habits. . . . His answers often express suspicion and evasiveness. When patient was approached by the writer he immediately asked for his release. He stated that he has been married to Margaret Truman in Washington and has written many letters to the former president. He is at loss to explain that he never met Margaret Truman and that he does not know where the wedding took place. When asked about his identification with Jesus Christ . . . he refused to elaborate on it. . . .

Less than two weeks later, he received his first electric shock: 140 volts to both temples, 0.75 seconds each. Since Mr. Zarchuk had no blood relatives in America, the Willard superintendent authorized the procedure. Questions of competency and informed consent were never raised.

Electroshock was quite popular in American institutions of the time. But was it reasonable to administer shock to a patient like Zarchuk, even according to the rather loose standards of the day? Probably not. Lothar Kalinowksi, one of the fathers of "electro-convulsive therapy" (ECT), held that "a well-preserved personality structure in a psychotic patient" is unfavorable for the treatment prognosis of ECT. Given what we know about Dmytre's life, he certainly seemed quite intact prior to losing his wife. And indeed, his "improvement" manifested itself in walking away from the institution.

A WHITE HOUSE CASE

The following special government form was placed prominently in Dmytre's chart, addressed to the Director of Willard State Hospital:

The United States Secret Service, Treasury Department, is interested in Dmytre Zarchuk who is now in your institution. We desire to be informed of subject's transfer or release, and therefore request that you fill out and mail the attached card (no postage required), in the event this person is to leave or has left your institution. As our file number on the attached post card identifies this person, it will not be necessary to insert any name on the card. IF THE ABOVE-NAMED SHOULD ESCAPE, PLEASE NOTIFY US AT ONCE BY TELEPHONE OR TELEGRAPH COLLECT.

—Special Agent in Charge

In psychiatric parlance, Dmytre was what is known as a "White House case," or a "Psychotic Visitor to Government Offices in the National Capital" (title of a 1944 paper by Dr. Jay Hoffman of St. Elizabeth's Hospital). Dmytre was unlike the many others who sought an interview with the president for a variety of unconventional reasons. Hardly anyone came to the White House with a love interest in mind, seeking to marry into the First Family or to become their adopted son. Most of the "White House cases" were middle-aged, single white men, and hardly any of them had lost a wife like Dmytre. Unlike the majority of "psychotic visitors," Dmytre had never seen a psychiatrist before his arrest. However, like a sizable proportion of Hoffman's original group, Dmytre came from an eastern European country, where the emperor or the tsar was known as Batiushka, "The Little Father of the People."

Dmytre already felt that he had a "personal" relationship to the president even before his wife died. When he hand-delivered his wooden model of the Utoropy church to the White House, he was already acting like one of the many petitioners who lined up to see the emperor every morning in front of the palace. His personal gratitude toward the president was a precursor to his attempt to marry Margaret Truman. Undoubtedly, this was an unusual way of coping with the sudden loss of a wife and an unborn child. Many people who find themselves alone in a foreign country far from their families develop peculiar relationships to authorities or places of importance. The anthropologist Anne Lovell, in her paper "The City Is My Mother," noticed how many homeless people on the streets of New York speak of their unique attachment to the city which plays a role in their personal mythology, surpassing anything their actual family might represent.

BILINGUAL CORRESPONDENCE

Dmytre had no intention of returning to his hometown Utoropy when he walked away from Willard in the fall of 1953. He wanted to see about his house in Syracuse and about getting his job back. Dmytre turned west toward the American Sector when he fled from a Soviet Displaced Persons camp, rather than face repatriation to the Ukraine. This and the fact that he visited the U.S. capital and the White House on several occasions shows a strong attachment to his new homeland, as a new immigrant who arrived here and never looked back.

The chart entry dated February 3, 1958, recounts Dmytre's renewed contact with his family:

In the middle of December [1956], the patient, for the first time, offered the wish to write a letter to his family behind the Iron Curtain. This letter was full of delusional ideas, including the statements that his wife has been murdered in an American hospital and that he is Jesus Christ. It was felt that the patient may benefited [sic] by correspondence from his family, and therefore, an additional letter was sent from the Director of the hospital to patient's mother. . . .

On December 5, 1957, Dr. Kenneth Keill wrote to Dmytre's mother, Mrs. E. Zarchuk:

This is to inform you that your son, Dmytre Zarchuk, was admitted to this hospital in May 1953. Our hospital is a mental hospital. This is the first time that Dmytre decided to write you a letter since he became sick. Possibly the first one since he left home during World War II. My intention is to give you some idea why it was necessary to hospitalize him and what is his present condition. After the death of his wife, Sofia, Dmytre suffered a nervous breakdown. His letter [not preserved] is almost self-explanatory. He still believes he is Jesus Christ and is persecuted just because of that. Our medical staff has doctors who speak Ukrainian and Dmytre is under the care of one doctor of Ukrainian descent. The latter believes direct correspondence between you and your son would be very beneficiary. Therefore I would suggest you write to him directly. . . . In case you would like to have some further information from our medical staff, do not hesitate to write. . . . Finally, I wish to inform you that your son is enjoying excellent physical health. . . .

A response was written by Dmytre's brother, Jurko Petrovych, on January 12, 1958 and was translated by Dr. Bohdan Huk:

Praised be Jesus Christ
Honorable doctor:
Would you kindly accept our sincere gratefulness for your letter and information. The letter we received contained both, the good and unfortunate news. The latter because of the fact that my brother is ill . . . this letter is written by his brother, Jurko. Your letter was addressed to our mother who died in 1947 and up to the day of her death, prayed and cried for her, she believed deceased, son Dmytre. Our sorrow is great as we learned about our brother's illness. But it is in the Hands of God what his future will be. You are our only hope. Please care for him and help him as much as possible. We know he is lonely, being far from us. . . . Honorable doctor, I and my two sisters, Nastja and Maria, will be anxiously waiting for your reply and further information. . . .

P.S. Honorable doctor, Zarchuk J. forgot to ask you to inform us, whether your patient, Dmytre, has any children. We also would like to have a photograph of our brother. Three photographs of our family, home and children were sent to Dmytre [not preserved].

Dr. Huk wrote a note dated February 3, 1958, shortly after receiving the brother's letter:

> On 1/21/58, an answer came from patient's brother, who showed an extreme interest in patient's welfare and at the same time proper insight into the condition of Dmytre . . . letters from the family are coming to the patient quite frequently since. Patient also answers the letters accurately and surprisingly to the undersigned never mentions his delusional ideas. However, during the discussion and interview, he does not give up his belief that he is Jesus Christ. . . .

The doctor was surprised that Dmytre censored his "delusional ideas" in communications with his family. Dmytre explained that "they were not educated enough to understand it." Dr. Huk countered by indicating that Dmytre "continues to be highly delusional, paranoid, kind of indifferent and very dull in emotional responses . . . [his] insight and judgment are absolutely lacking, although he is oriented in all 3 phases and coherent in his verbal productions. . . ."

What happens when a patient tells his psychiatrist that he is Jesus Christ, but keeps this a secret from his family? Why do some patients act so much crazier during the day shift, when they are surrounded by doctors and other staff, but keep it together during social hours, picnics, or at nighttime? Could it be that the context determines the experience and expression of madness? Dmytre was held against his will in a psychiatric hospital, had attempted to walk away from there, kept trying doorknobs to see if there might be an escape, and yet he did not seem to have the wherewithal to convince the psychiatrist of his sanity. He wrote letters to the police, the Red Cross, to the president and his daughter, asking them to believe his story and to help him get out of the hospital. Whenever he talks about being Jesus Christ, he says it in a rather peculiar fashion. For example, Dmytre's letter to the Syracuse police dated January 31, 1958, shortly after the arrival of his brother's first letter, opens with "Proud of Jesus Christ!" and goes on: "I did write to Policeman Syracuse N.Y. about that that Syracuse N.Y. arrested me for nothing for that that I am Jesus Christ." The opening clearly echoes Jurko's words "Praised be Jesus Christ" and may be Dmytre's poor translation of this Ukrainian devotional formula. Maybe he was trying to say that he was innocent like Jesus Christ. He was arrested like Jesus Christ "for nothing," and he was suffering (in the hospital) undeservedly like Christ. "And now I have something other . . ." he goes to tell the story about his wife's admission to the hospital, her operation and her death, which he attributes to the work of bandits, who are also after him "for that that I am Jesus Christ and do not have an excuse . . . to live." And, remarkably, in the next sentence, he says:

"My wife too some bandits kill for that that she was Jesus Christ. Do not have an excuse on me arrested me for that that I am Jesus Christ and will not leave me from here." For Dmytre, "being Jesus Christ" may have been another way of saying that he and his wife were innocent, that she did not deserve to die, and neither did he deserve to end up in a mental institution. A psychotherapist would have used this analogy to help Mr. Zarchuk, but for Dr. Huk, this letter was just more proof for the seriousness of his mental illness. And Dr. Keill relied on Dr. Huk's opinion when conveying this information to Dmytre's family.

An inquiry by Dmytre's sister Nastja arrived on March 10, 1957:

Dear doctor, please inform me whether my brother is really mentally ill, whether it comes to him only periodically and whether he is under continuous treatment or perhaps he just works in the hospital.

Dr. Keill took this as an opportunity to elaborate further about Dmytre's condition:

. . . Our records indicate that Dmytre was married to Sofia Jaromij in 1946 in one of the International Refugee Organisation Camps in Austria. While there he took some educational courses and established a trade as an electrician. On March 22, 1949, Dmytre and his wife entered the United States and established their living in the city of Syracuse, New York. . . .

He goes on to tell them about the down, payment for the house, the gift of the model church to President Truman, and Sofia's death "following the complications from a miscarriage," and continues:

Shortly thereafter, Dmytre began to feel an extreme persecution and in this respect his life resembled to him the life and sufferings of Christ. He felt that in the United States everything is possible and, therefore, he developed a delusional idea that he was in love with Margaret Truman, whom he considered Mary Magdalene. On four occasions in 1951 and 1952, Dmytre visited the White House in Washington in order to tell President Truman about his Christ-like condition and about his love for the President's daughter.

In this letter, Dr. Keill exhibits a rather keen understanding of the circumstances that led to Dmytre's psychiatric admission. But his empathic grasp never reached the patient under his care. Instead of receiving treatment that would have reflected this intuitive understanding, Dmytre was locked away and shuttled between various bleak and bleaker hospital wards.

HOSPITAL JAIL

In 1959, Dmytre's fellow patients "were given the privileges of an 'open ward,'" but Dmytre was not deemed fit for such freedom and was transferred to another locked unit. A year later, Dr. Huk still thought that he showed "extremely poor judgment" and completely lacked insight. He kept him confined, feeling that Dmytre would use "the first chance he gets to run away from this prison." Dmytre refused to work in the occupational therapy shop, feeling exploited "because they wanted to make money on jewelry boxes."

> *In general he is quite careless, although tidy in his personal habits. He spends his time sitting idly in a rocking chair, watching other patients and employees, and occasionally writes a letter of complaint to the Police Department in the city of Syracuse. It is felt that the patient is hallucinated in the auditory sphere, although on direct questioning he denies the same.*

Two years later, he was again transferred, this time to a "Research Unit for . . . possible retreatment or social service planning." But another two years passed without any positive developments for Dmytre. His new Swiss psychiatrist, Dr. Adolph Hug, did not speak his language and condemned him as a "paranoid, far deteriorated schizophrenic with a poor prognosis," doubting whether he could ever live outside the hospital. This opinion was largely based on Dmytre's response to the question about why he was at the hospital: "Cayu (neologism) Russia Ukraina before over 400,000 miles large dig big hole 4,000 machines all destroyed Christ." This doctor did not speak Ukrainian, yet he decided that one of Dmytre's words was "a neologism," the invention of a deluded mind. Verifiably, a huge swath of land with a majority of Ukrainian-speaking people was incorporated into the Soviet Union after 1917, with little sympathy for their Christian beliefs. In 1940, Stalin put together nine divisions with a thousand tanks each to confront the Germans who had pushed through the Ukraine and advanced beyond Leningrad. More than a million soldiers participated in the Soviet counteroffensive beginning in January 1944. By then, Dmytre had already been captured by the Germans and was working on an Austrian farm. It is possible that his sympathies lay with the Germans against the Soviets, who had put a "big hole" into the heart of his country and who challenged the Ukrainians' Christian beliefs. Even if Dr. Hug was right to consider Dmytre's answer gibberish, could it have hurt, in the spirit of "retreatment," to take his actual concerns seriously, like being imprisoned in the hospital, or his wife being murdered by unknown conspirators, and about his homeland being the victim of two wars waged by huge armies on its territory?

OCCUPATIONAL THERAPY

Dmytre did get a second chance. On February 27, 1964, he was brought back to the Intensive Retreatment Unit because he had shown "some talent for drawing and painting." By the time he met his fifth psychiatrist, Dmytre had begun "doing serial paintings about the events in his life, particularly how he immigrated to the United States and some of his impressions of the prison camps during World War II and the German Army." He was doing this work with the guidance of occupational therapists Nancy Jaycot and Murray Olmstead, himself a painter. While his new doctors deemed Dmytre to be a regressed schizophrenic who should never leave the hospital, his occupational therapists had a rather different impression:

> *DZ is most co-operative in his OT projects and shows an unusual artistic talent. His watercolor paintings and linoleum block prints are beautifully done. He organizes well in his projects, and anticipates supplies needed, and co-ordinates production. . . .*

Dmytre Zarchuk painting in Occupational Therapy, c. 1960

Initially, Ms. Jaycot saw him as rather isolated and unwilling to accept suggestions, but within a few months Dmytre apparently "became more aware of other people and somewhat more receptive . . ." The first time he sold one of his paintings (for two dollars), he bought a "selection of candy and distributed it to all other patients and employees in the ward dayroom." Ms. Jaycot emphasized the "severe language barrier" that hampered her client, and the fact that Dmytre did not hallucinate while working on art, but "immediately after class . . . he sits alone and grins, liable to laugh aloud and rock to and fro."

GOING HOME

Unlike most of the suitcase owners, Dmytre Zarchuk did not die at Willard. In fact, he lived for twenty-seven years "in the community" without ever again seeing the inside of a psychiatric hospital. How did he manage to get out? What distinguished him from all the others who spent their final days at the institution?

For many years, Dmytre was considered an escape risk and someone likely to spend the rest of his life in a hospital. It is hard to discern why he was not deported to his home country. Quite possibly, cold war politics were not favorable for the repatriation of a person with a "mental illness" to the Soviet Union. The correspondence between Dmytre's family and the superintendent did not lead them to believe that taking him back home would be advisable. Instead, they became convinced that Dmytre was best taken care of in an American mental institution, which they were never likely to see. In a letter dated June 17, 1958, his brother inquired if Dmytre could be "returned to our home and country," if he would be able to travel by himself, and "would the return . . . to his family (he is extremely homesick) be beneficial for him or vice versa, [as] the new circumstances could throw him into a more serious mental condition." Then Jurko adds:

> I have to mention that I am just a poor farmer and I know that whatever I may do for him, I will never be able to give him the comfort he is given at your dignified institution. Do you think he will be greatly disappointed when he sees our misery to which, however, he was adjusted before? On the other hand, he would not have the adequate medical supervision and care, and I would like to know whether he is in need of such. We all would like to welcome our brother and fulfill his wishes, but we would never want to be the ones who participated in further regression of his mental condition, and, therefore, we just cannot make any decision without your advice.

Unfortunately, Dr. Keill's answer is not in the record.

Nearly a year later, Dr. Keill informed the family that "all the treatments we have tried, unfortunately, have failed, and it appears impossible to change his mind." Here, Dr. Keill refers to the fact that Dmytre was no longer writing to his family, apparently because he believed they did not answer his most recent letter. Dr. Keill surmises that "he is slowly developing an idea that you are plotting against him with the authorities of our institution and do not intend to help him return to the city of Syracuse, New York." This was certainly not encouraging news. Maybe Dmytre was homesick for Syracuse and not for Utoropy. He was apparently hoping that his family could help him get back to the home he made for himself as a grown man.

The family did not give up. They continued to send letters of inquiry, until they finally received a more definitive answer to their questions from Dr. Keill:

> *It might be possible that while at home and in the surroundings close to his heart, your brother might get more active and perhaps decide to participate in activities or work. As far as his basic mental status is concerned, this I don't believe will be changed even after his return home. Most probably, he will remain extremely suspicious, delusional, and use very poor insight and judgment. I am quite certain that after a short period of time, he would be antagonistic toward you, the rest of the family, local government, and the doctors in case it is necessary to give him medical treatment.*

FAMILY CARE

By 1961, when this letter was written, many state hospital patients were receiving recently introduced drugs such as Thorazine and Haldol. Dmytre was not given any psychiatric medication until 1971, when Thorazine concentrate—50 mg, three times a day—was prescribed. However, the doctors did not think it made much of a difference and stopped the medication less than a year later. Dmytre kept busy in occupational therapy, completing at least one painting a day, until he joined the "compensated workshop" where he put together jewelry boxes and was rated as "one of the fastest piece workers now employed in the hospital," making himself a few extra dollars per week.

The occupational therapy notes show a gap between March 1968 and June 1971, when he was transferred to another building. Apparently, he had developed a problem holding his urine, which made it difficult to keep himself clean. This, too, is often a sign of prolonged institutionalization. In September 1971, a psychiatrist concluded that "his condition is not sufficiently improved . . . to consider placement in the community." Less than a year later, a different psychiatrist came to the opposite conclusion, suggesting that Dmytre would be "a good candidate for family care or a nursing home."

Family care is one of the oldest community mental health programs. It involves placing a person with a psychiatric diagnosis in the home of a specially selected and trained lay family. Its origins go back to the Belgian town of Gheel, where thousands of former patients live in the homes of some of the town's three thousand families. The nearby shrine to St. Dymphna, the patron saint of the "mentally ill," attracted thousands of pilgrims over the centuries. The citizens offered their homes as sanctuaries to anyone so afflicted, with a great deal of success. By the 1930s, New York State had begun to follow the Belgian example on a much smaller scale. Each state hospital developed its own program and a small number of patients moved into private homes, doing chores and being monitored for symptoms and problem behaviors. On March 1, 1976, Dmytre Zarchuk was accepted into the Willard Family Care Program.

During the seventies, Dmytre was not idle. He made $32.64 every two weeks as a trucker's helper. According to his supervisor he "functioned extremely well," was "cooperative, dependable and very helpful" in this position. Once Dmytre was placed at the family home, he was allowed to keep his job in the garage, and he received a brief course of molindone, a brand new drug, for supposed hallucinations, but the hospital quickly ran out of the drug. Dmytre stayed in this home less than six months. The family sent him back because he had problems holding his urine at night, and because he used tools surreptitiously to fix up his room.

When Dmytre was brought back from Family Care, he returned to his hospital routine, working in the garage and whiling away the rest of his time in a rocking chair. In April 1977, twenty-four years after his admission to Willard, a Department of Mental Hygiene Resource Agent wrote to Dr. Keill:

> *I researched the deed recorded June 22, 1950 for Dmytre Z. and found that the property was conveyed on March 28, 1952 to a Myron Spewack. . . . Please inform Dmytre that since he sold the property to Mr. Spewack he no longer has any interest in it.*

The mystery of Dmytre's house in Syracuse was finally laid to rest. Apparently he sold it to his friend Myron Spewack, who kept in touch with him for many years while in the hospital, and brought him a Ukrainian Bible when the state's agent could not find one. Until 1977, Dmytre still believed the house belonged to him. Possibly, the evidence that the change of deed was entered into the official record finally convinced Dmytre that he could never return to his house, and that he would be better off accepting an alternate placement.

PERMANENT DISCHARGE

Following his return from Family Care, the staff began to see him as a suitable candidate for the Tompkins County Home in Trumansburg, New York. During a lunch visit there in March 1977, Dmytre met a woman who spoke only Ukrainian and he helped translate her statements to the charge nurse. Apparently, Dmytre enjoyed this visit and agreed to move to Trumansburg, thirty miles from the hospital. He had to give up his job at the garage, and the hospital took the $1,295.37 from the sale of his house to Mr. Spewack as reimbursement for his six-month stay in Family Care.

Sending a man like Dmytre to a former poorhouse closes a circle that started in the mid-nineteenth century, when state hospitals where built for people deemed insane who were languishing in almshouses. The original Tompkins County poorhouse was closed in 1947 after almost 140 years of operation. Twenty years later it was resurrected as a "home" for people with psychiatric histories, when hospitals no longer seemed appropriate (or cost-effective) environments for them. As institutions go, this rural home was rather pleasant and may have suited Dmytre's expectations. The two-story clapboard building with porches and wainscoting faced several big old trees and a couple of acres of farmland. Dmytre lived there for 10 years and had little contact with mental health services. He had spent almost 25 years in a state hospital at a substantial cost to taxpayers. The monthly cost of state hospital care was approximately $3,000 and steadily rising; 25 years would add up to something like $900,000. Once he was no longer thought to need hospitalization, he was sent to a place that cost less than a third of the hospital rate. It is moot to think that investing only a fraction of this money in the house that Dmytre had built might have saved him from this experience, and the public coffers from a great expense. In the community, he might have found work and provided for his own livelihood. In the hospital he contributed free labor, offsetting the bill for his care by a certain amount.

In the summer of 1987, Dmytre again came to the attention of psychiatric authorities when the county home administrator called in the Geriatric Mobile Team for an evaluation. Dmytre had become quite upset, "acting out, ranting and raving," when he learned that the home was scheduled to close and that he had to move again. The "screening/admission note" states that Dmytre had been washing dishes at the home and spent most of his time writing. His physician had recently prescribed a low dose of the drug haloperidol, apparently without "any discernible improvement."

The evaluation recommended a doubling of the medication dose and a referral to another family care home. The psychiatrist found very little out of order to report. Allegedly, Dmytre's "judgment, especially around the issue of leaving the county home, was poor." After the years of shuttling from ward to ward, from Family Care back to the hospital, from one Displaced Person camp to another, from one Syracuse address to another, Dmytre might have felt that the Tompkins County Home had become his final abode. But once again, for reasons beyond his control, he was uprooted.

In 2001, one of Dmytre's former social workers told us that Dmytre had moved to a place called Preston Manor in nearby Chenango County. It turned out that Dmytre had been one of the most cherished residents of this rural facility, home to forty-eight former psychiatric patients. Preston Manor was also a converted poorhouse from the 1830s. It gave Dmytre another chance at joining a family of peers and providers, not unlike the life he might have led in his hometown, had he returned there. Of course, there he would have found his brother and sisters, their children and grandchildren, and he would have lived within the bosom of his native culture. The entire village would have been his home and he might have been Uncle Dmytre to quite a few of its inhabitants.

At Preston Manor, Dmytre painted and wrote steadily. His mural on the dining room wall reflected his favorite subject—the place he called home. As a twenty-nine-year-old refugee, he had found the love of his life less than a year after crossing from the Russian into the American sector.

Mural by Dmytre Zarchuk, Dining Room, Preston Manor, Oxford, NY, 2002

Sofia's dark features and serene smile still beckon from the pages of their wedding album, made of handcrafted paper with an Alpine farmhouse on the cover and a heart carved into its windowpane. Amost forty years later, at the end of his life, Dmytre had made enough of an impression to be remembered by all who met him for his gentle wisdom, his helpful, artistic nature, and for the person he was, not a "mental patient." He had finally found a home.

10.
MY BLOOD TEMPER
. . . RESIGNED

The Brooklyn neighborhood of Bedford-Stuyvesant, north of Flatbush Avenue, appears much the same today as it did in the years around World War II, when Frank Coles rented rooms in several of its patrician brownstones. Standing on Jefferson Avenue, it is easy to imagine a different set of cars parked in front of the row of neatly trimmed front yards and three-story buildings, some possibly still inhabited by descendants of Frank's former landlords.

Among the attic dwellers, Frank Coles stands out for several reasons. He was the only African American identified as a suitcase owner, an army veteran who served during World War II. The event that sparked his commitment was remarkably trivial, especially considering that it led to life-long incarceration. One day he had lunch at the Virginia Restaurant, down the street from where he lived. His food was served on a chipped plate and he didn't like it. He left the place and took out his anger on a garbage can at the street corner. Someone called the police, and they hauled him to the precinct and from there to Kings County Hospital, a gargantuan medical complex that takes up forty city blocks just south of Bed-Stuy. He didn't like talking to the doctor either, but nevertheless shared that he felt angry, upset, and disrespected at the restaurant, and also that he was fed up that he had not been with a woman in a long time. When the doctor asked him about his relations down in West Virginia and Ohio, he finally broke down crying: "I know that I am at the Kings County Hospital. I am not sick. I got excited on Fulton Street and I was throwing garbage. My blood temper, it went up. I was angry. In the Virginia Restaurant I got a broken plate. I thought that someone planned to kill me. I stayed by myself most of the time. Could not understand the broken plate. I do not get enough to eat for some reason. Something inside me takes all the good."

Why did a broken plate upset him so much? Was the waitstaff at the restaurant white or black, female or male? Why should anyone want to kill him? He kept mostly to himself, lonely, yearning for female companionship. He may have seen the broken plate as a warning that the food was poisoned. Whatever he ingested, it did not nourish him enough since he felt hungry, starved as a man. "Something inside him took all the good." What kind of notion is that? An inner creature that robs a man of the essential nutrients, the juices of life. Madness and folklore are closely linked. A man losing his mind might offer explanations that are totally outside common human experience. Food is often subject to fears and spiritual beliefs. Many people feel poisoned when their sexual juices back up. Certainly, the admitting psychiatrist in the Kings County hospital emergency room did not share such "low culture" beliefs. It was much easier for him to rank these tales among the symptoms of a mental illness: The term *paranoid schizophrenia* was easily pronounced; everything was seemingly explained by this diagnosis, even though the patient had not been to a psychiatrist in years. He had been working intermittently and had never been hospitalized, despite his medical discharge from the army, suggesting that his troubles may have been with him for quite some time. His ideas of reference—the chipped plate indicating danger, bizarre delusions, all the good is being sucked up inside of him, paranoia, thinking people want to kill him, disordered thoughts, jumping from one subject to another within a sentence without a clear logical connection—could be fit into the vast concept of schizophrenia, and was indeed taken as such by the admitting psychiatrists.

Records from Kings County Hospital are missing, but a clinical summary from Willard provides an excellent picture of the way the doctors thought about Mr. Coles when he first presented himself. On the Observation Ward, he was noted to be: "emotionally unstable, idle, with periods of impulsiveness and restlessness, suspicious of others, evasive, and his insight and judgment were impaired." Almost immediately, he was given a diagnosis of dementia praecox, paranoid type. By the time he was sent from Kings

County to the adjacent Brooklyn State Hospital, a mere two weeks after the garbage-can incident, he was considered certifiably mad by a local judge, therefore suitable to become a ward of the state.

Paranoia and paranoid schizophrenia are diagnoses more commonly given to African American men than to any other group. Many interpret this as a form of racial stereotyping—the "suspicious, violence-prone black man." And as in most of these situations when there is such a rush to judgment, Frank had not shown any violent proclivities prior to his admission. By the time he arrived at Willard, about nine months after his apprehension, he was deemed incurably insane. Four years later, his treating psychiatrist reported many details that revealed Frank's state of mind, but this did not cause him to reconsider the diagnosis of dementia praecox, which had been out of style for at least twenty years. The doctor's words reveal quite a bit about his thinking of Frank, and the impossibly obtuse logic by which psychiatry operated.

> *Mentally, on admission, patient's productions were limited. There was some degree of spontaneity in his attempt at expressing his difficulties, but his thoughts were restricted chiefly to the incident that led to his hospitalization, so that memory of this shut off some consciousness on [sic] other episodes of his life.*

Why would it be surprising to the doctor that his patient was still preoccupied with the day of his arrest less than nine months ago? It was probably one of the most dramatic and consequential incidents of his life. Yes, he had been given a medical discharge from the Army, but it did not land him in a mental hospital without legal recourse. And, as we now know, the memory of major traumatic incidents tends to overshadow a person's life before and after the incident rather considerably.

"Relevancy, continuity, and logic in the thought [sic] is lacking"—in other words, whatever Frank was talking about was irrelevant to the doctor, and the way he expressed himself did not make any sense to a well-educated New York psychiatrist. Lacking a transcript of the conversation, we can only go with the available material, presented entirely from the doctor's point of view:

> *Emotional reaction—depressed, mildly agitated, especially when he resorted to frequent crying spells . . . he was apathetic, somewhat fidgety and restless, as he sat on the chair and wished to create the proper impression with physician and constantly regretted having to cry, and as he called it to annoy examiner.*

Leaving aside the numerous contradictions—"mildly agitated," "apathetic," "fidgety and restless"—it becomes obvious that this doctor was dealing with a very despondent man who was quite distressed about his predicament, while at the same time trying to maintain a modicum of composure. None of this swayed the doctor in any way.

Frank's sexuality apparently played a major role in the way he was feeling. If he talked about loneliness early on, he certainly elaborated on this theme further, as quoted by the doctor:

"I have lots of courage. I didn't have a girl for seventeen months. My face was round, full of blood from eating too much food. That's what got me upset too. You got to have a girl. . . . I always feel lonely. I have wet dreams lots of time. I had one a few nights ago." Again, the theme of sexual energy backing up, filling the body with excess blood and leading to rage. Somehow, food had something to do with it, too, but there is not enough information to understand the way he connected these experiences.

In the clinical summary that accompanied Frank's transfer to a Veterans Administration Hospital in 1949, Dr. Gutheil mentions an incident from his patient's stay at Kings County Hospital:

> . . . he became disturbed with no apparent provocations, required sedation and restraints . . . he explains his aggressiveness by stating that the fellows [on an all male ward] were annoying him, that they were sitting next to him, and that he doesn't care for men to sit near him at any time.

Homosexual fears were once considered a hallmark of paranoia, and Freud proclaimed that homosexual conflicts are at the root of every paranoid psychosis in men. In the context of Frank's professed intense desire for sex with women, it seems odd that he was so rattled by males rubbing up against him, metaphorically speaking. But then again, frustrated sexuality may indeed have caused him to feel less than a man, and thus threatened by his fellow patients, some of whom may actually have been seeking a homosexual encounter.

The psychiatrist came to a rather damning conclusion: "in spite of the little data available at this time, there is nevertheless no doubt that his reaction is that of a malignant type of psychosis in the form of schizophrenia."

How did an apparently healthy, good-looking man turn into a "malignant schizophrenic" at the age of thirty-four? Had he been symptomatic for years without anyone noticing his symptoms? Aside from his medical discharge from the army, no information was found that might shed light on this question, but there are some clues about the kind of life he led before his hospital admission.

Frank Coles worked most of his adult life. Up until 1944, he drew a salary from L.A. Carlin, a Brooklyn company, and also worked for Leo H. Hirsch on Second Avenue in Manhattan. These seem to have been just occasional jobs. Nevertheless, he deposited a steady sum of $50 every other week in his checking account throughout 1944, and also maintained a safe-deposit box. This enabled him to pay his rent uninterruptedly, which ranged from $16 to $20 per month. Most likely he worked off the books, possibly as a chauffeur.

Something happened in the summer of 1944. His deposits dropped from $50 to $13, and then to an occasional dollar deposit by the end of the year. Maybe he lost his job, or merely didn't bother depositing his income, as there was no lapse in his rent payments up until the day of his admission. But he did move frequently. Between the spring of 1943 and the summer of 1945, he lived at four different addresses, all within a radius of a few blocks.

Frank's last address outside of a hospital was on a quiet block in Bedford-Stuyvesant, surrounded by churches and prayer rooms, just a block away from Fulton Street, which today is again the bustling shopping area it was during the 1940s. From his perch on the top floor of a three-story brownstone, he would have had a clear view down to the corner of the Virginia Restaurant.

Little is known about his life prior to his arrival in Brooklyn. There are some hints that he first landed in Harlem, like many African Americans who made their way to New York from points south and west. Born in Ohio, he chose New York over West Virginia, where his parents and siblings had moved during the Depression, possibly drawn by the fairly steady work in the coal mines. If he lived in Harlem, he may have joined the many Harlemites who followed their church and community leaders to the cheaper and less crowded new developments in Brooklyn. Bed-Stuy was a bedroom community for people working in the city, its large brownstones providing ample lodging for boarders, both single men and women.

Frank kept working through the Depression years, first as a chauffeur, then as a laborer, as his papers attest. For some reason, his belongings included mostly materials from 1940 on. Given how meticulous a collector he was, we can only assume that much of his earlier stuff had gotten lost along the way, never making it to his last address, from which everything was shipped up to Willard.

The year 1940 was a watershed year for Frank Coles. In April, he was terminated from an eighteen-month position as a laborer with the Federal Works Agency (FWA), due to a mandatory time cap on employment. He was living at 263A Bainbridge Street with his girlfriend Pauline, and probably struggled to find another job. Later that year, he was admitted to Kings County Hospital for ten days and underwent an unidentified operation. In early February 1941, he was granted a chauffeur's license by the local board, but rather than use it locally, he decided to enlist in the army and joined the motor pool at the Field Artillery School in Fort Sill, Oklahoma.

Presumably, he wanted to upgrade his license so he could drive big equipment in his new uniform. Frank made it "one year seven months and fourteen days" as a soldier in a Black Unit, according to his own records, with only a few days' discrepancy from his official discharge date of October 15, 1942. The reason given for his honorable medical discharge was a mental disorder. Most soldiers diagnosed with a mental disorder separate from service within one year of enlistment. Frank certainly outlasted this statistic, but nothing more is known about the kinds of troubles that led to his honorable separation. The date when he was declared "unfit for duty due to a mental condition not suitable for military services" was four months before his actual separation. Quite possibly, he had recourse to protest this decision, suggesting that it was an insidious rather than an acute problem that prompted this determination, or perhaps he was hospitalized while still on active duty. Remarkably, the only records that remain from his service at Fort Sill are two permits granted to spend a weekend in the nearby city of Lawton, Oklahoma. Did he keep those for accidental or sentimental reasons? Were they visits by his girlfriend Pauline? Other family? These are unanswerable questions, although he did return to live with Pauline on Bainbridge Avenue in the fall of 1942, once again facing the prospect of unemployment.

Losing his FWA job, the unidentified surgery, and his medical discharge were three major incidents that set the stage for Frank's further decline. Needless to say, none of these incidents were considered particularly relevant by the psychiatrists who treated him in following years. The role of life events in the onset and course of a psychiatric condition was neglected until the mid-1960s, but has fallen out of favor again since the "Decade of the Brain" was declared during the 1990s.

When did he apply for a Coast Guard ID, stating "I'm tired of doing nothing"? Was it after his stint in the army or before? We don't know. Why did he open a safe-deposit box in Brooklyn only days after his medical discharge finally came through? Was he counting on an Army pension, or did he anticipate coming into cash that he did not want to appear in his savings or checking accounts? Again, these are unanswerable questions. Frank was not successful in obtaining his medical records from the army (and neither were the authors, after several protracted attempts). Between collecting unemployment and obtaining short-term work, he managed to survive the winter of 1942–43, then registered with the New York City Department of Welfare and let his chauffeur's license lapse. It seems that Frank rented a place around the corner from Bainbridge Street in April 1943, no longer sharing an apartment with Pauline. It comes as a bit of a surprise, given his precarious financial situation, that he and Pauline traveled to Ohio during the summer of 1943. From postcards in his trunk, it appears that the couple met up in Cincinnati, his hometown, arriving there from different directions.

On December 12, 1943, Frank received a Western Union telegram with the lapidary note: MAUDE C._ DEAD COME OR WIRE IMMEDIATELY signed JOE C. Below this Frank made a handwritten note: "Leaving ~~Monday~~ Tuesday night if possible no later." In his meticulously kept notebook, he made the following entry, apparently copied from the funeral announcement: "Service for Maude C., 58, Carbondale who died Saturday will be held at 2 P.M. tomorrow at the Mount Zion Church at Carbondale. Rev. W.C. Gregory Sr. will officiate. Burial will be in Woodland Cemetery at Cedar Grove. The body will be removed at 5 P.M. today from Harden Mortuary in Montgomery to the Residence." Frank was present when they took his mother's body across the Kanawha River to the family church and then upstream to her final resting place at Cedar Grove, deep in coal mine country.

No further dates appear among his papers until sometime after February 22, 1944, when he received a postcard from his brother Carl and his wife, Alice, who referred to herself as "Sis." "Hello Frank/Thought we would write and let you hear from us. We are up here with my sister. Carl is gonna get a job. Hope you are getting along fine," signed: Alice and Carl. This was the beginning of a correspondence with various family members, mainly his father, Joe, his sister-in-law Alice, and his sisters, Lena Chatham in Williamson and Nannie Scales in Cinderella, West Virginia. Maybe Frank was indeed getting along fine. But piecing his life together retrospectively, we can see that more trouble was on the way. In his admission interview at Willard, Frank stated that he had not been with a woman for seventeen months, which would have made January 1944 the approximate time of his last sexual encounter. Did he and Pauline break up once and for all at this time? He apparently did not connect with anyone after that date.

The IRS was after him for a tax return and the Veterans Administration threatened to hold up his mustering-out checks unless he filled out some additional questionnaires and sent in his discharge certificate for scrutiny. He did manage to straighten out his VA business and checks started coming in late April. Meanwhile, his father, who was ailing and still mourning his wife, began to lean on Frank for money. Frank was meticulous about recording his expenses and account balances, but we don't have the entirety of his records. He didn't have much, but apparently he helped his father out whenever he could.

Things took a turn for the worse in the summer of 1944. His father was hospitalized and needed surgery, Frank missed the chance for a job with the postal service, and by September, he changed addresses once again. To make sure his mail always followed his moves, Frank sent penny postcards and registered letters to himself, in addition to filing the usual change of address

forms. More letters from his father arrived at his new address, beseeching him for financial help, while he himself could not have been doing very well. In November, an ominous letter arrived from a psychiatrist, Dr. Bianchi, at Brooklyn State Hospital, requesting that Frank appear for an appointment only three days after the postmarked date. From later correspondence, it appears that he did not keep that appointment. Clearly, the VA had an interest in making sure that Frank showed up for this psychiatric evaluation, as they wanted to determine his continuing eligibility for his pension. Dr. Bianchi was less than clear in his communications with Frank, suggesting, on February 5, 1945, "Please do not report for examination until you hear from me. I shall have to wait until I receive your record before I can examine you." In the meantime, Frank had received a letter from the VA threatening that his pension would be suspended unless he kept his appointment with the doctor.

In the winter of 1944–45 Frank moved twice, staying at each address only two months or less. Both of these buildings are still standing: 350 Jefferson is a respectable brownstone with alcove apartments, and 330 Hancock was recently renovated in the course of the rapid gentrification taking place in Frank's old neighborhood. He did not lapse in his rent payments, which ranged from $14 to $20 every four weeks, even though his finances must have taken a direct hit in the fall of 1944. The average balance in his main savings account went down from $50 in June to $10 in

October. What prompted him to spend at least one night at the YMCA in February 1944 is unclear, but since he had already moved twice that winter, he might indeed have been short of cash at times. On March 3, 1944, he paid $16 to Mrs. Warner for a room at 135 Decatur Street, only one block from where he stayed when he first came to the neighborhood.

On the last Sunday of May, he picked up a copy of the Sunday *News* and kept the cover for his wall. The war had ended three weeks earlier, and the paper showed a triumphant FDR on its cover. On the inside were photos of German POWs and their activities, as well as a story about the opportunity of becoming a bus driver ("30 hours of classroom instruction, paid $13.50 a month for part-time work; of 4,810 buses students operate over 3,800"). These stories must have resonated with this former soldier and commercial driver, now out of work and unattached in his lonely mansard room.

Less than a week later, he became a prisoner of the mental health system, never to emerge again. Willard did nothing for him other than get him transferred into the custody of the Veterans Administration, which is why the staff went out of their way to have his belongings shipped up to Willard, hoping to find his discharge certificate there. For bureaucratic reasons, it took them three years to accomplish a transfer to the Canandaigua VA Hospital where Frank spent a decade or more. The VA system did not emphasize discharge at that time. Even more than state hospitals, the Veterans Administration believed it appropriate to keep its psychiatric patients indefinitely, well into the age of the so-called psychopharmacological revolution. Not until the 1990s did the census of VA psychiatric hospitals go down dramatically, and then only due to a change in policies rather than advances in treatment. Aside from one index card that noted the dates of his transfer from Canandaigua VA to the Pittsburgh VA, no other records could be found, even though every conceivable personal identification number was used. Frank had kept a careful list of all his service-connected numbers.

We don't know if Frank ever reconnected with his family, if his brother and sisters even found out where he had ended up, and whether his transfer to Pittsburgh had anything to do with being closer to his relatives. All we know is that he died there in 1986, in his seventy-seventh year, after spending more than forty years in various institutions. What happened to the suave amateur boxer who was obviously a ladies man, as the many photos of beautiful women in his picture collection attest? What happened to the meticulous, neat, sharply dressed, and rather self-assured young man who kept on top of his personal troubles, his finances, and his family's needs? Did madness set in one day in the spring of 1945 and ravage his mind without provocation? The answers to these questions will remain as mysterious as the man who wore the perfectly folded uniform.

Once he arrived at Brooklyn State Hospital, Frank's first stop in a series of long-term institutions, he began to break down. "Attempts to cooperate well and apologizes repeatedly for his crying spells." Somehow the doctor got the impression that he was out of work for several years due to a lack of sexual relations. He also notes a great deal of dejection, "self-pity and a feeling of rejection and neglect on the part of others." In the midst of this sadness and depression, in spite of which he was "doing a great deal of work on the ward," Frank suddenly became agitated and "required sedation and restraint." This episode was apparently set off by some male patients getting too close to him. A few days later he was given the diagnosis of dementia praecox, paranoid type, and promptly transferred to another building "to create a vacancy." On the new ward, his sexual concerns become even more apparent. He claims that people called him a fairy and that men in the park flirted with him.

The chart entries by the psychiatrists over the next few months are virtually identical. Aside from repeating psychopathological terms such as blocking, ideas of reference, paranoia, defective insight and judgment, and hallucinations, he was noted to be a good worker and more pleasant and agreeable than before. Less than a year after his arrival at Brooklyn State, he made the trip up to Willard. There, the chart notes get even sparser; there was not even an admission note, as would be customary. Instead, a small testicular mass was noted, and a lawyer from the Veterans Administration reportedly made inquiries. Nothing was written about Frank between April 9, 1946, the date of his arrival, and July 3, 1948, when a physical examination was done. Two weeks before he was shipped off to Willard, he was said to be "causing trouble at night when there is little supervision," and allegedly attacked other patients. The diagnosis of dementia praecox went along with him when he was transferred to the Veterans Hospital at Canandaigua, New York, but his belongings stayed behind. If not for his trunk, we would never know about Frank, about the kind of ladies man he was with dozens of pictures and addresses, or what kind of amateur boxer he was, and what kind of heavy machinery he drove for the Negro Contingent.

On February 20, 1948, a social worker by the name of Anderson visited the home of Mrs. N. Warner on Decatur Street to inquire about Frank. Mrs. Warner was laid up in bed, but told the worker that Frank's possessions were still in her basement, and that she had not shipped them up to Willard as requested, since they needed to be packed. Mr. Anderson returned a few days later and found "one trunk (Army locker style), locked, no key, and contents undetermined. Also a laundry mailing case filled with clothes, and a duffel bag also containing clothes, toilet articles, shoes and letters." He packed additional clothing, suits, and a raincoat into the duffel bag and left a card with the patient's name and address for the express company to ship. They called the next day.

Less than nothing was done for Frank at any of the hospitals he was shipped to. Chart notes tell of a man who became increasingly withdrawn, was obviously despondent and fearful, with no one bothering to find out what was troubling him. Frank spent only three years at Willard, as long as it took to secure the documents needed for his transfer to a Veterans Administration hospital. Evidence of a meticulous and simple lifestyle turned up in his trunk and duffel bag: an army uniform, clean and neatly folded; shirts; laundry; underwear; polished shoes; socks; and boxer's hand wraps. His personal mementos, photographs, letters, and

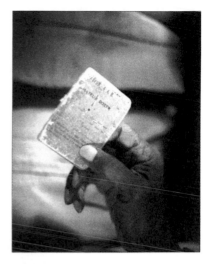

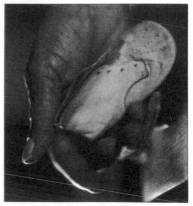

diaries underscore that he cared about other people as much as about himself. He kept a list of relatives and their addresses, telephone numbers, dates of birth, and a very moving letter to his father, which he probably never mailed.

What happened to the anger he brought with him? Did it simply recede with perpetual neglect? As one of the very few black inmates of the time, did he fall prey to racist attitudes in an institution almost exclusively run by white staff?

11.
AN ITALIAN PRINCESS
AND A FRENCH
INTELLECTUAL:
TWO WAYS OF FIGHTING
FOR FREEDOM

Although born on different continents almost two decades apart, Madeline Cartier and Irma Medina had a surprising amount in common. Beauties in their youth, they were sophisticated single women from respectable families who immigrated to the United States in the early twentieth century. Both lived in Manhattan in the 1920s, partaking of its rich cultural and educational opportunities, and each used the city as a base for her far-flung travels. Madeline taught French literature in private schools and took classes at Hunter College and Columbia University, while Irma worked for the venerable French perfumery Roger et Gallet, gave private French lessons in her spare time, and was involved in the musical world of New York.

Madeline was born in 1896 to a wealthy Parisian family of brandy distillers and arrived in New York from Le Havre in 1920 on the ship *Rochambeau*. Irma, eighteen years Madeline's senior, had an Italian father and a French mother and was born in

Irma, c. 1915

Madeline, c. 1921

Alexandria, Egypt. She sailed from Genoa on the *Prinzess Irene,* arriving in New York in 1910. As self-reliant women, both earned a decent living for many years. But when the Great Depression struck, both became destitute, and their lives took tragic downward turns that eventually brought them to Willard State Hospital on the same day in 1939.

As educated single women who came from countries with relatively few immigrants to the United States, Irma and Madeline were unusual among early twentieth century immigrants. Between 1910 and 1920, more than 60 percent of immigrants arrived as part of a family group; the largest numbers came from Ireland, Italy, the United Kingdom, and eastern Europe. Less than a quarter of single immigrants at the time were women, the vast majority of whom lacked formal education and found work as domestics or factory workers. Unlike most of their sister immigrants, Madeline and Irma initially lived comfortable and intellectually stimulating lives in their adopted country. Yet both eventually lost everything and found themselves in what must have been unthinkable conditions for women of their backgrounds, confined for decades on overcrowded asylum wards, without contact with the outside world, and with nothing to look forward to.

THE FRENCH INTELLECTUAL

"The false is so mingled with the truth, and looks so like it that there is no sure mark whereby we may distinguish one from the other. It is a damned fool of a world."
—*Inscription in a book in the handwriting of Madeline Cartier*

Beyond the fact of her birth in Paris in 1896, little was found in Madeline's trunks or records concerning her childhood. As an adult, she was estranged from her family. She told the admitting psychiatrist at Bellevue, where she was first hospitalized in 1932, that her parents had died and left her a large sum of money before she came to the United States. This statement is contradicted by a 1936 letter in her file from the chief medical inspector of the New York State Department of Mental Hygiene, stating that the American consul in Paris had contacted Madeline's father, who, it was reported, "can not care for her in his home and does not desire her repatriation to France."

As the only child of a wealthy couple, Madeline's childhood was likely one of privilege and comfort, but there is no way of knowing about the emotional environment of her home. A gifted student, she graduated from the Sorbonne at age twenty-one, and in the years after World War I, traveled in Europe and the United States. In her trunk were dozens of photographs documenting her trips and her life in the U.S., where she settled permanently in 1920. One packet of photographs records a trip to Lake George, New York, and beyond with a group of friends, showing Madeline canoeing and hiking with a guide in

Madeline, Paris, c. 1905

the Adirondacks in 1917, when such a trek would have been still something of a wilderness adventure. Another group of pictures depicts a transatlantic voyage on the ship *Britannia* from New York to Marseilles in June 1921, with stops in the Azores, Portugal, Spain, and Gibraltar. She traveled back to France several times during the 1920s, but always returned to New York.

Why Madeline chose to settle in the United States, working first as a secretary at a special French mission on war bonds, and later as a French literature teacher at private girls' schools, remains a mystery. Perhaps she had worn out her welcome at home and needed to earn her own living; unfortunately her possessions hold no clues as to why she decided to do so in the United States. Some sense of the twelve years she spent in this country before she was hospitalized in 1932 can be pieced together from the contents of her trunk, the many photographs she kept, what she chose to tell the various doctors who examined her, and from letters to, from, and about her found in her medical records and among her belongings.

sur le faîte de Cobble Hill (à gauche White face mountain)

C.S.A

Septembre 1917

"*On the trail at Cobble Hill (White Face Mountain to the left).*"

By all evidence, she was a smart, active, independent woman with a certain sense of entitlement; she had an outgoing personality and made many friends. There are photographs from her years in New York showing her at parties, sailing with friends, skating in Central Park, and as a house-guest at impressive homes in sub-urban Westchester County. Her date books show numerous lunches with woman friends, dinner parties, and attendance at readings, lectures, and concerts. While there are photographs of Madeline with various gentlemen, nothing in her papers mentions a romantic relationship with any of them, so that part of her life, too, remains a mystery.

Indien et sa femme (américaine)

U.S.A

Au pied de "White face Mountain" Sept. 1917

"*(American) Indian and his wife. At the foot of White Face Mountain.*"

Vigo, Spain, 1921

Madeline aboard the Britannia, *Gibraltar, 1921*

In her writings, she refers to her "dearest friend, Mrs. Hartshorne," and there are a number of letters and cards in her trunk, including some sent while Madeline was in a state hospital, from Sarah Moore Hartshorne. Some of these letters mention mystical experiences and the spirit world, subjects that later figured in Madeline's commitment to a psychiatric hospital.

The clothing found in Madeline's trunk was elegant and well-made, including a beautiful silk gown with fine lace inserts, spoiled when her name and ward number were crudely written on it in black ink. She also owned a cane with a carved duck's head as a handle, a golf club, an espresso pot, several pairs of fine kid gloves, and red leather-bound date books for the years 1923 to 1931.

> *24800.168 Dress, silk satin, peach color, Straight neck line with three flat tabs approximately 3" at shoulder, no sleeves, skirt gathered to bodice, snap closure at both sides at waist. Self-fabric roses are stitched at waist. Cream colored lace (net and spider web design) panel with tuck gathered at each side and snapped at waist across opening. "M. C— /45" written in ink at back neck, bleeds through to right side Condition: good—fraying at hem, stained under arm.*

> *24800.265a, b   Riding Habit, Wool and leather, khaki colored twill weave, light weight. Very nice tailoring. a—riding pants, leather (dark suede) at inside knee area, six buttons at calf, waist closure—three button placket closure each side, front waist watch pocket, seams are finished with dark brown bias tape. b—Coat, princess line seams front and back, simple lapel, full skirt, knee length, three buttons at bodice and two buttons on skirt which button to flaps and are hidden from the front, pocket in side seam with decorative stitching on outside, breast pocket on left, three buttons at cuff of long slender sleeve with cuff angled & topstitched in place, lined with ribbed twill, back tails lined with stiff sized fabric. Label at center back neck woven, crest in orange, lavender, black and cream "En tete/ Franklin Simon & Co./ Fifth Avenue, N. Y."; label tape sewn over this "M/ C—." Condition: Good some moth damage and minor staining.*
> *24800.167 Blouse, gold lace in leaf pattern, square neck and narrow cap sleeves, double layer at neck so appears to have a yoke at neck, decorative stitching at neck and sleeves, label at neck "M. C– 45"*

The many books found in Madeline's trunk point to her intellectual interests: volumes of philosophy, poetry, literature, and psychology in English and French. Her papers included essays written for classes at Columbia University and Hunter College, where she studied with the

renowned literary critic Lionel Trilling. Among them was an eight-page typed paper entitled "The Greatest Soldier and the Greatest Lover of His Time," an analysis of unpublished love letters between Napoleon Bonaparte and the Empress Josephine, along with several ring binders and folders of her notes from lectures on literature, psychology, and philosophy. She had an interest in classical music and probably played the piano, as her trunk contained sheet music by Schumann, Mozart, Beethoven, and Debussy, among others.

While Madeline's social life and her scholarly pursuits flourished in New York, maintaining steady employment became increasingly difficult. After losing her job at the French mission on war debts, she worked for a time at a French bank in New York. With the help of an employment agency, she found work teaching French literature in a succession of private schools for girls, but did not stay at any one post for very long. She taught in Dallas, Boston, St. Mary's School in Peekskill, New York, and later at an Episcopal girls' school, Stoneleigh Manor, in Rye Beach, New Hampshire, whose imposing stone buildings and lovely gardens are featured in a number of photographs from 1928 and 1929.

In 1932, Madeline found work at the Oak Knoll School in Summit, New Jersey, where she commuted from New York. During the spring term, she was quite ill with whooping cough for several weeks. The school at first hired a substitute for her, but later sent her half of her semester's pay and a note saying that her services were no longer needed. This precipitated a rapid decline in her finances and her emotional state. She lost her housing, and, like many other unemployed people during the Depression, turned to the government for help. Finding her unemployable due to her emotional distress, the Emergency Work Bureau helped her secure a series of furnished rooms over the next several months. But like her employers, the landladies, too, found her difficult, and often asked her to leave. The Work Bureau followed up with a referral to the New York Psychiatric Institute for outpatient treatment. The Institute, established in 1895, was one of the first institutions in the United States to integrate teaching, research, and therapeutic approaches to the care of mental patients. It was also among the few clinics that offered free outpatient services. During this time, Madeline was also arrested and briefly detained for trying to charge a meal at Schraft's to a French businessman, a blunt illustration of her dire financial circumstances.

Madeline's emotional problems emerged over several years as she became more deeply drawn into the world of mystics and psychics. She believed that she could communicate with certain people through what she called "psychic association," mutual telepathic exchanges that she sometimes found disturbing. Letters in her trunk from several doctors counseled her to ignore these unusual phenomena. As early as 1928, her friend Sarah Moore Hartshorne had gently warned her to tread carefully in pursuing her interest in the supernatural:

> *I see by your letter that you are troubled and I wish we might talk rather than touch so mystical a subject by pen alone for I am afraid of your misunderstanding my attitude toward the world of the spirit. The spiritualism that expresses itself in table rappings through mediums and other occult agencies has always been very repellant to me and I have kept away from them. It opens a wide gate for impostors.*

With the onset of whooping cough, Madeline became ever more frantically concerned with these "psychic associations." She experienced so powerful a bond with the Rev. Dr. Robert Norwood, pastor of St. Bartholomew's, a Park Avenue church, that when he died in 1932, she was completely bereft. St. Bartholomew's began as a huge parish house on 42nd Street, built with the support of the Vanderbilt family, ministering to large numbers of immigrants who lived in appalling poverty in the tenements of the East Forties and Fifties. The parish house included a gymnasium, laundry, print shop, employment bureau, loan association, health clinic, and social clubs. A chapel provided diverse forms of worship in several languages. Under the leadership of the Rev. Dr. Norwood, the church moved into its new quarters on Park Avenue and 51st Street in 1918. Madeline may have joined the parish sometime during the 1920s. A poet and prophet, Norwood was a dynamic preacher who brought large crowds to the church week after week.

In the fall of 1932, Madeline's writings took on a desperate, sometimes unfathomable tone. Apparently, her doctor at the New York Psychiatric Institute felt she needed more help than he could provide and referred her to Bellevue for evaluation, stating that she had "a far advanced case of schizophrenia." Madeline believed she was going there to consult with doctors doing research on psychic phenomena, and when she found herself committed to a locked psychiatric ward, she was furious. In a matter of weeks, she was transferred to Central Islip State Hospital on Long Island, where she appeared "excitable and dramatic" and demanded her immediate release. Outrage with her confinement was to become the central theme of her forty-seven-year stay within New York's state hospital system.

A MUSICAL LIFE

"I had a wonderful life, up until seven years ago."
—*Irma Medina , upon admission to Central Islip State Hospital, 1933*

Among the contents of her trunk and in the transcript of her intake interview, there are tantalizing clues about Irma Medina's twenty-three years in New York prior to her commitment to Bellevue's psychiatric ward in 1933. They paint a picture of a fairly well situated woman from a colorful background who made friends among the wealthy, was involved in the musical scene in New York, and who eventually became unmoored due to unemployment, homelessness, situational crises, and a growing sense of paranoia. Both women's lives show that a privileged upbringing and a work life as an adult do not necessarily protect one from emotional upheaval under dire economic circumstances. Neither Madeline's formidable intellect nor Irma's cultured demeanor could ultimately stave off their social decline and the determination by psychiatrists that both suffered from the same purported condition, paranoid schizophrenia.

Irma's origins and youth are even less well-documented than Madeline's. She told doctors at Bellevue and Central Islip that she was born in Alexandria, Egypt, in 1878, and that her father was Italian and her mother French.

Irma, c. 1915

Why her parents settled in Alexandria or what her father's occupation was remains unclear. Europeans living in Alexandria during that period tended to be either merchants or artists, so it seems likely that her father may have been a businessman of some kind, as the family was apparently well off. An intriguing photograph found in her trunk shows seven Caucasian adults in elaborate Victorian outfits on camels posed next to the Sphinx at Giza with the Great Pyramid of Cheops in the background; a young girl, perhaps age ten, sits on a donkey, while a tiny Egyptian boy holds the camels' reins. The people in the photo are not identified, but one wonders if the girl on the donkey is Irma and if her parents are among the adults pictured.

She told doctors that her father died in Egypt and her mother remarried before Irma came to the United States in 1910. Her Ellis Island record indicates that she lived in Cairo before she embarked for the U.S. at age thirty-two. She graduated from high school at age eighteen and attended college for a short time, "but then I had to come home." Where Irma started college or why she dropped out remains a mystery. She may have spent some time in Paris, as her trunk contained a num-

The Sphinx and the Great Pyramid at Giza, c. 1890

ber of items, including sheet music, that were purchased there. What is clear is that Irma embraced music for much of her life, most likely as a pianist, and possibly as a vocalist, too. Her trunk contained almost 150 pieces of sheet music for solo piano and bound volumes of music purchased between 1891 and 1930. Her taste was quite eclectic, including classical composers such as Beethoven, Schumann, and Brahms; music from Mexico and South America; much operatic material; and a host of popular songs from the 1910s and 1920s. One such piece of sheet music, "Love's Calling: A Twilight Serenade by Jack Bauer," was inscribed "To Mlle. Irma M.—The best French teacher in N.Y. Sincerely yours, Jack Bauer."

A clipping from the journal *Musical America*, dated September 15, 1917, headlined "Jessie Baskerville Relinquishes Music to Direct War Relief Work," mentions that Irma was one of several women associated with the Metropolitan Opera who helped prepare bandages for shipment to France in the workroom that Miss Baskerville financed and oversaw. Jessie Baskerville was a noted operatic coach at the Metropolitan Opera, and must have been a personal friend of Irma's, as her home address and phone number were written in her address book. The exact nature of Irma's association with the famed opera house is unknown.

24823.70 Sheet Music "El Choclo/ Tango Argentino/ by/ A. G. Villoldo"

24823.71 Sheet Music "Moonlight Sonata/ (Sonata Quasi Una Fantais)/ L. Van Beethoven/ Op.27 No.2"

24823.81 Sheet Music "Indian Love Call/ words by/ Otto Harbach/ and /Oscar Hammerstein 2nd/ music by/ Rudolf Friml" published 1924

24823.197 Choicest/Mexican Music/ The Swallow La Golondrina Fantasia A. F. Heckle; Copyright 1891, "Miss Irma M—" written in pen at the top of the cover

24823.204 Divertissement/ des/ Esclaves Persanes/ extrait/ du Roide Lahore/ Acte II /par/ J. Massenet; stamp on second page indicates this was purchased in France

Irma's address book contained the names of many women with Park Avenue and Upper East Side addresses. Perhaps she met them through the Metropolitan Opera, her work at the perfumery, or as students who engaged her for private French lessons. In 1925, she accompanied Mrs. Cornelia Covert Meyer, the wife of a major real estate developer, on a three-month tour of Scandinavia. Her trunk contains photographs, postcards, and travel guides to Denmark, Sweden and Norway. Irma wrote a lengthy travelogue of their trip in French, apparently in hopes of publication. The preface of the manuscript states Irma's intentions:

> *I am only a humble writer. I will not attempt to write like the great authors, telling neither the formation nor the history of the Scandinavian countries, but briefly the little I saw and visited in the course of three months. The readers who are interested in knowing customs of the country, the different climates, the different natural beauty will get a clear picture without needing to travel. I dedicate this book to Mrs. Cord Meyer, an American woman from New York whose charming family is well known. Her knowledge of museums, ancient and contemporary history go beyond that of an amateur. Despite her huge fortune, her maternal heart was even greater during our trip.*

Mrs. Meyer's husband and father-in-law, both named Cord, had essentially created the community of Forest Hills in Queens, New York, at the turn of the twentieth century. The Meyers lived in a waterfront mansion in Great Neck, Long Island, named The Cove, which was enough of a local landmark to be printed on postcards of the day. Irma was close enough to the family that she had their private telephone number in her address book.

One wonders why her wealthy friends did not offer some assistance when she became destitute just a few years after Irma and Mrs. Meyer traveled in style throughout Scandinavia.

Her trunk held evidence of her refined taste in clothing and accessories:

24823.3. *Black and Purple Dress: ca 1920–25 Designed as a robe and approximately 48" in length. Mauve at the top and black from waist downward. Sleeves and neckline have a purple ribbon at the border. Patterns of black and purple thread hand embroidered in floral pattern around waist covering both colors. Bodice lined in purple silk faille. Small piece of cloth stitched, as a tag, in the back with "I.M—" written in ink on it. Material is wide Corduroy. Condition: good but evidence of moths.*

24823.9a b. *Chinese Slippers: Golden/Yellow with colorful floral embroidery on the shoes. Thin and narrow. Chinese characters written in black ink on the leather sole stitched to upper of the shoes, flat with almost no heel. "MADE IN CHINA" printed on paper glued to inside of shoe with characters above and below, Chinese character printed in red on muslin lining of shoe. Label printed inside bottom of shoe "the Oriental Store/ Benjamin E. Palmer/ jewel and / imported from the orient/ China Japan India Persia/ 261 Fifth Avenue New York/28th Street"*

24823.137 *Shawl c. 1920: Long net and silver, white color. Netting ground. Small silver pieces bent around netting in decorative pattern. Row of trees at each end and row of people above that, small crosses cover rest.*

Irma worked for many years in the New York offices of Roger et Gallet, a venerable Parisian perfumery established in the sixteenth century when its owners were bequeathed the original formula for *eau du Cologne*. The seeds of the decline that eventually led to her commitment were sown in 1926, when she began to suspect that the perfumery was being used as an illegal distillery to manufacture whiskey during Prohibition. This seems plausible, as there was certainly money to be made from bootlegging during those years. Major Chester Paddock Mills, prohibition administrator for the New York City district from 1926 to 27, suggested that 98 percent of bootleggers' supplies came from the diversion of industrial alcohol. "Suppose, for example, that a manufacturer of perfumes has a permit to possess large quantities of denatured alcohol. Were he dishonest, he might sell this alcohol, labeled as 'perfume,' to an equally dishonest wholesaler. Then the wholesaler sells the 'perfume' to a bootlegger, who re-distills the alcohol and uses it, sparingly, in the making of intoxicants." Consequently, Major Mills recommended closer inspection of permit holders such as perfumeries and closer supervision of their activities.

While Mills's assertions were probably exaggerated, they did not get him labeled as "paranoid." Irma, on the other hand, informed her friends and the police about her suspicions and was promptly fired from her job. She was furious, and believed the perfumery was being allowed to continue its illegal activities because of its political connections. She became convinced that a high-ranking officer of the firm was having her followed and wanted her deported.

Unable to find another office job, she taught French for two years at Miss Rochefort's girls' school near Columbia University. When she could no longer afford her own apartment, Irma, a devout Catholic, boarded at various convents. She lost her teaching post in 1928 and picked up work as a chambermaid in a series of Manhattan hotels over the next few years, struggling to stay afloat. She continued giving private French lessons and took shorthand courses in French and English to improve her job prospects.

Irma's fixation on the perfumery scandal may have interfered with her work as a chambermaid. She was fired from one hotel for alleged rudeness to a guest, and from another when some valuables disappeared from a guest room. Eventually, like Madeline, she found herself unemployed and was set up with furnished rooms by the Emergency Work Bureau, which paid her rent of $1 per week. Irma continued to look for work; her trunk contains handwritten drafts of letters describing her skills in French and shorthand, a handful of letters of recommendation from some of her wealthy friends, and the rejection letters she received in reply.

The Emergency Work Bureau placed her in a temporary public service job at the Bronx Botanical Gardens in 1933, where she translated scientific articles from French and Italian. In October of that year, her landlady evicted her because of "queer behavior," which included sitting by the window all night, not sleeping, convinced that she was being watched from the street. Irma found herself with no place to go but to a municipal lodging house, much like an urban homeless shelter of today. What happened there is not spelled out in the commitment papers, but on October 31, an ambulance was called, and Irma was escorted to Bellevue. Less than two weeks later, she was committed to Central Islip State Hospital. She was fifty-five years old and about to begin her thirty-eight-year confinement within the state's mental hospitals.

BEHIND LOCKED DOORS

The two women's lives in New York City seemed to run on parallel tracks, but their time in mental hospitals converged unexpectedly. And yet Madeline's and Irma's responses to being diagnosed and confined could not have been more different. Each was quickly transferred from Bellevue to Central Islip; Madeline in 1932, and Irma a year later, where she joined Madeline on Ward 55. They stayed on that ward together for several years and were certainly acquainted with each other, although both were noted to be reclusive and highly selective in their contacts with other patients. Despite their difference in age, both were well-educated, spoke French, and had an interest in music, so they might have found each other compatible company. Since medical records rarely include information about patients' relationships with one another (unless they are violent or otherwise troublesome), it is impossible to know whether they became friends.

Irma's admission photo

Madeline's admission photo

Madeline felt that her commitment was a terrible injustice and was in high dudgeon throughout her five years at Central Islip, writing frequent letters to her lawyer demanding that he secure her release. She did not receive any reply and assumed that the hospital never posted her letters. She also wrote to friends and acquaintances, begging their help to get back to Manhattan. Some

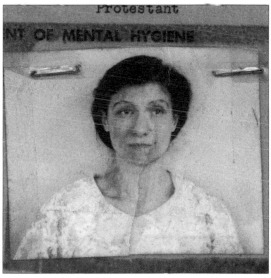

responded with admonitions to follow the doctors' orders, while others inquired with the hospital superintendent, who invariably replied that Madeline was much too sick to be discharged. She wrote frequent complaints to the superintendent about the violation of her rights and demanded to be released to attend classes at Columbia. All these letters were compiled in her record as further evidence of her insanity.

Irma, on the other hand, was "quiet, agreeable, well-behaved, and easily managed" for the first two years at Central Islip, but her medical record said that she "has no insight into her condition and is resistive to the development of any insight." Initially she was seen as a good worker, but by 1935 she had become more "sullen and withdrawn," refused to do any work, and felt that the staff and other patients were against her. She retreated into a fantasy world, believing herself to be an Italian princess named Leticia from a wealthy family in Naples, married to a Count Ladislaus.

Irma was transferred to Kings Park State Hospital on April 6, 1937; Madeline followed a week later. From her two years at Kings Park, Irma's record contains only three notes, all commenting on her lack of insight, her refusal to work, and her belief that she was an Italian princess. Madeline's file contained just ten notes during the same time period, mentioning that she refused to work, spent a great deal of time reading, and that she persisted in her belief that she was being confined illegitimately and repeatedly demanded her release.

> JUNE 17, 1937: *Patient [Madeline C.] received today on Ward 41 from Ward 120. She was somewhat restless, wandering about the ward but when questioned answered promptly and relevantly. Stated that she was being detained here without cause, that she was quite well enough to leave and get a position. Her manner was quite superior and she talked in an affected and manneristic way.*   —M. Evans, M.D.

> SEPTEMBER 14, 1938: *She complains a great deal when seen on rounds and during the interview. She requests continuously that she be permitted to go home. Her productions are spoken with a strong French accent and are concerned mostly with her complaint that she is being kept in the hospital unjustly, that she does not have enough clothing and that she is not accustomed to such a life as she is leading in the hospital at present.*
> —I. Portnoy, M.D.

THE END OF THE LINE

Irma and Madeline were among a large group of patients transferred to Willard from Kings Park on May 1, 1939. A steady flow of patients was sent to Willard from overcrowded downstate facilities during that period. People came on buses carrying twenty-five or more, usually accompanied by a doctor, a nurse, and several attendants. They were often shackled during the trip, which took the better part of a day. People were not given notice of their impending transfer, nor any explanation; they were simply loaded onto the bus and driven away. Witnesses reported the bewilderment of these urban people who stepped off the bus and found themselves in a massive institution in the middle of nowhere. Realizing this, some of them decided to run, but there was nowhere for them to go. The entire area was inhabited by Willard staff.

THE ITALIAN PRINCESS

The first note in Irma's Willard record was entered five months after she arrived:

Irma, 1937

OCTOBER 4, 1939: *Since patient was transferred here from Kings Park State Hospital at first she was quiet and cooperative causing no disturbance whatsoever but was markedly seclusive, irritable and aloof, showing very little initiative. Within the past few weeks, however, she has shown decided assaultive tendencies toward other patients. Because of dangerous tendencies she is today transferred to Ward 5.*
—Dr. Walters

Ward 5 on the South Wing of Willard's main building was one of the feared back wards for patients who were considered most troublesome; these wards had a reputation for neglect, filth, and violence. A former attendant who worked on such a ward said that "the ward service was dark. The lights had no shades, they were just bare bulbs hanging out of the ceiling. They were sixteen foot ceilings and in the winter time it was so cold that if you took a glass of water and put it on the windowsill in one of the dormitories, it would freeze before the eight-hour shift was up. And it was boring and it was dangerous. It was dark and it was cold and it was stinky and I hated it. I hated it. I enjoyed my interactions with the patients who weren't trying to hurt me. The rest of the time I felt like I was, you know, in danger and alone and unappreciated." If the staff felt that way, one can only imagine how the patients felt.

Irma, 1950s

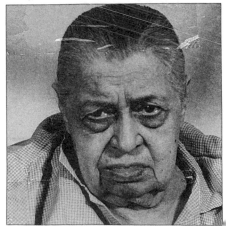

Irma, 1960s

In 1942, Irma was transferred from this dreadful place to a smaller building called The Pines. She was no longer seen as assaultive, but still believed herself to be Princess Leticia and felt surrounded by enemies trying to cause her harm. She went to work in the laundry, where, coincidentally, Madeline also worked. Irma remained at the Pines for the next sixteen years; for two years, she and Madeline were on the same ward. Irma's chart says that she avoided other patients, feared her enemies would try to kill her during her sleep, kept calling herself Princess Leticia, and was generally irritable and unhappy. In 1952, when Irma was seventy-three, Dr. Shreier noted that "she refused to give her name, fearing that some harm will come to her by giving information about herself. . . . She appears to be totally oblivious to her environment and lives in her world of phantasy and unsystematized delusions." He also discovered that she was diabetic and started her on insulin injections. In the mid-1950s, like the majority of Willard patients, Irma was started on the new drug Thorazine, and kept on one such drug or another for the rest of her life, with no improvement in her mental or emotional state.

In 1958, she was transferred to a newly created ward for diabetic patients. In one of the mostly perfunctory chart entries, the writer records Irma's beliefs about her royal origins, as well as her statement that she came to the United States on the ship *Prinzess Irene*, which the writer considered equally "untrue" as her belief that she was Princess Leticia. Irma was offered no psychotherapy and participated in no activities, spending year after year sitting on the ward by herself. As she aged, her health grew worse, and she spent much of her last nine years in Willard's infirmary. There she was considered "quiet, seclusive, uncooperative, disagreeable, but doesn't cause any management problems." Irma died on April 10, 1971, at the age of ninety-two, and was buried in the Ovid Union Cemetery nearby. The record states that she had no known relatives or friends, and her clothing was donated to patients on another ward.

"WILL FIGHT FOR HER FREEDOM"

Unlike Irma, Madeline never accepted her fate. For decades, she considered her confinement a grave injustice and was never hesitant to express her opinion.

OCTOBER 25, 1939: *This patient is usually quiet. She spends all her time sitting on a chair; does not mingle with the other patients. However, she reads a great deal and observes very closely her environment. She is fairly neat and tidy in her appearance and habits; she eats and sleeps well. Whenever spoken to she at once becomes irritable and suspicious and demands in a very aggressive manner her release. Usually replies to any questions, "I refuse to answer such silly nonsense!" Her sensorium is clear and she is oriented in all fields. Insight completely lacking.*

—Dr. Kern

NOVEMBER 19, 1943. HALLUCINATED, PARANOID, ORIENTED, PHYSICALLY WELL

This patient recently contacted the local Episcopal minister, Rev. Henderson, asking if he could initiate some procedures to gain her release from this hospital. He inquired of the Director, Dr. Keill, as to her condition. As a result patient was today interviewed. She reviewed many of the incidents connected with her admission to Central Islip and her transfer to Kings Park. She believes that people were against her and talked about certain people involving her by psychic associations. When questioned further on this point stated these associations were a form of mental telepathy. She has no insight into her past or present condition and does not see why she is being held in this hospital. She states she would like a teaching position but will not do menial work. She is well oriented, her memory appears intact, she reads a great deal and listens to the radio. It is believed that this patient's mental condition would interfere with her adjustment out of the hospital and furthermore she has no known relatives in this country who are interested in her. A trial placement in Home Care might be attempted if the patient were willing to go but she refuses to leave the hospital under such a plan. —Dr. Strong

JUNE 9, 1952: DELUDED, IDEAS OF GRANDEUR, BELLIGERENT, WILL FIGHT FOR HER FREEDOM, POOR JUDGEMENT, NO INSIGHT

This 57-year-old patient of French descent speaks with a decided accent but fluently enough to make herself understood. She is fully oriented but very argumentative and convinced there is nothing wrong with her mind. She has always been seclusive, never married nor manifested any adjustment to reality. Her ideas of grandeur appear to compensate for her inner weakness. She keeps herself aloof from the other patients and has not found any social contacts here. Physically she appears well.

—Dr. Schreier

MARCH 22, 1965 SUMMARY AND MENTAL EVALUATION *[excerpts]*

At today's interview we see a frail old woman with a shriveled, wizened face, narrow eyes, prominent teeth, a stiff and sarcastic smile frozen on her face. Interviewer remembers that at several chance previous encounters with this patient she only shouted hostile remarks at him and insisted in a preemptory manner that the medication which he ordered be immediately discontinued. She still refused to answer questions concerning

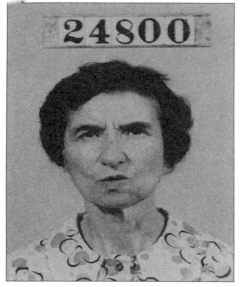

biographical data, stating: "You have my full record, why do I have to answer all these questions?" Patient has preserved a sense of humor and she laughs heartily when explained that this was a typical answer of paranoid patients. She continued: "I don't like this hospital, I resent being detained and wasting my time. I was always in good mental health. Since you are around, my intellectual capacities are weaker. I have to take medication twice a day which is detrimental physically."

—K. Feuchtwanger, M.D.

Madeline after receiving neuroleptic drugs, c. 1960

Madeline was correct about the detrimental effects of the neuroleptic medications—Mellaril and Trilafon—prescribed by Dr. Feuchtwanger, more correct than she probably even knew at the time. The doctor's description of her "shriveled, wizened face, narrow eyes" and the "stiff and sarcastic smile frozen on her face" were signs of an irreversible movement disorder called tardive dyskinesia (TD), which was caused by the drugs. In the months and years after, other notes mention that "Madeline shuffles or dances-like on her feet when talking to anyone or when she stands," "she exhibited extreme grimacing and various twitchings of the hands, arms and trunk," and that she had "slight mannerisms about mouth and gait of a stomping nature," all symptoms of TD. In 1970, social workers considered placing Madeline in Family Care, the practice where patients were boarded with a family in their home. "Her continual fidgety movements, rigid stances, and facial grimaces" were considered an obstacle to such placement. In 1975, Madeline, then seventy-eight years old, was sent to "behavior modification therapy" in an effort to stop the movements and grimaces so she could be placed in Family Care. This was clearly a pointless exercise, given that the neurological cause of these movements were not within her control.

One is tempted to excuse as ignorance the staff's persistent attempts to modify a behavior caused by their treatment. Tardive dyskinesia and similar iatrogenic disabilities were first documented in the psychiatric literature in 1973, although these conditions had been observed (but not named) as early as 1958. The psychiatrists who first introduced neuroleptics noticed rather quickly that the drugs caused symptoms not unlike Parkinson's disease, but saw this as evidence that the medication was working effectively, rather than as an indication that it caused neurological damage. Dr. Feuchtwanger had certainly not heard about tardive dyskinesia when he noticed Madeline's twitches in 1965, and instead of lowering the dosage, prescribed an additional neuroleptic drug. But by the time Madeline was sent to behavior modification therapy in 1975, the psychiatric literature had acknowledged the existence of TD. Nevertheless, decades later, when the full extent of the problem had become quite obvious, psychiatrists continued to prescribe these drugs for most patients in institutions, despite their limited effectiveness and the disfiguring and disabling side effects. For patients like Madeline, there was no way back once they had been exposed to these drugs. After several years, she, like millions of her peers, was in the same predicament: she had become dependent on the very medications that had caused these neurological symptoms.

Despite Madeline's persistent movement disorder, she attended a typing class, one of the few activities she apparently enjoyed. During 1972, she took pleasure from weekly visits by a French-speaking volunteer from Cornell University. Otherwise, the notes covering her last decade at Willard were strikingly similar, asserting that there was no essential change in her condition.

Madeline was sent to North Brook Proprietary Home in Auburn, New York in 1975 and placed on "convalescent care" status. This was not exactly a discharge from Willard; she remained on their rolls and Willard's outpatient staff directed her treatment, visiting her regularly for several years. According to the record, the staff at North Brook "affectionately" called Madeline "Frenchie." One wonders how "affectionate" this nickname actually was, as the entry goes on to state that "If she has not endeared herself to the staff she is certainly well known to them because of her perseverance and strong willed independence."

AUGUST 2, 1979: CLINIC VISIT
This is a 78 [sic] year old, white, female patient who has been here for the last three years. She seems well adjusted to the environment and there is no evidence of gross psychiatric symptomatology. Therefore, she is being discharged on this date. —Antonio Lugue, M.D.

With this brief note, Madeline finally regained her freedom after forty-seven years of struggle, but it was rather a Pyrrhic victory. Living in a board and care home in an unfamiliar town, with no money and no friends on the outside, she had little chance to make an independent life for herself. And since no notes were made in her file after her formal discharge from Willard, we do not know how she spent the last seven years of her life. Madeline died in Seneca County, New York, in October 1986 at age ninety; her burial place is unknown.

EPILOGUE:
IS IT BETTER TODAY?

*Isn't there something that could be done
for us: A job, a home, get a life?*
—Board-and-care home resident, 2006

Are the lives of people with psychiatric disabilities better now than during the time when the people profiled in this book were kept for years at Willard? Do they have a better chance of being listened to empathetically, are they offered a choice of humane and effective therapies, is there a realistic chance of them regaining control of their lives? The common wisdom is that major advances have been made in the mental health field in the last sixty years, largely credited to psychotropic drugs, but a closer look at the evidence paints a bleaker picture. While many fewer people now spend decades in state mental institutions, problems such as poverty; trans-institutionalization in prisons, nursing homes, and large board-and-care facilities; medications of questionable efficacy and disabling side effects; and the revolving hospital door now rule the lives of millions of Americans with psychiatric disabilities. The Willard stories are still relevant, as thousands enter our nation's mental health system every day, with limited chances of emerging unscathed, or even improved. If hospital stays are considerably shorter, due to the aggressive use of medications, the limitations imposed by insurance payers, and the availability of more community housing, they are no more marked by recovery and full community integration than in the days of the large state hospitals.

At its peak in 1955, the census of state mental hospitals in America was 559,000. In 2007, there are about 57,000 state hospital beds nationwide with around 240,000 admissions annually. So clearly, many fewer Americans are now institutionalized for years, but this is not entirely a thing of the past. Victor is a forty-four-year-old man who has spent most of his life in New York State psychiatric hospitals. He was sent to a children's facility at the age of four after being removed from his parents' home, where he was sexually and physically abused, and has lived outside of a hospital for a total of only five years since then. Victor described life on the wards in terms reminiscent of the conditions under which the suitcase owners were kept more than fifty years ago:

> *Nobody cares about anybody. None of these programs here are at all beneficial or helpful. They're designed to keep a patient hospitalized so they can learn how to function within the facility. They don't orientate you into the community. This is supposed to be a temporary holding spot until you're ready to go back in the community, but yet, over half the population has been here five or more years. That is something that needs to change. It's inhumane to take a person who has a breakdown, bring him in, put him on medication and strip him of his dignity and hope and his self-respect for the rest of his life. Many cases like that in here. Being trapped in a system with no way out.*

As state hospitals were closed and downsized over the years, many people were diverted to the psychiatric wards of general hospitals or to private psychiatric facilities. In 2002, there were almost 1.5 million admissions to these facilities in the United States. For many, a first hospitalization is the beginning of a lifelong career as a mental patient. Today, out of every hundred people admitted to a psychiatric unit, more than sixty will go on to a life of largely unremitting mental distress and exclusion from the mainstream of American life, despite the widely touted new drugs.

TRANS-INSTITUTIONALIZATION

Since the early 1960s, money has been steadily if slowly diverted from mental institutions to community-based services. For many people, this has led to being moved from one kind of institution to another, not to community integration. In 2003, more than 103,000 people in the United States lived in congregate care in places like group homes or board-and-care facilities, large buildings filled with former inpatients that are tucked away in undesirable neighborhoods. About 300,000 people with psychiatric diagnoses (other than dementia) were living in U.S. nursing homes in 2004, and more than 1.25 million of the nation's state and federal prisoners and local jail inmates in 2006 had serious mental health problems.

None of these environments is particularly conducive to healing from emotional distress and becoming fully reintegrated in society. Life in group homes and privately owned board-and-care facilities, for example, is not too different from life on a psychiatric ward. Residents lead very circumscribed lives in these segregated facilities. They are bused in vans bearing official insignia to day programs that offer few meaningful activities, brought back to their residence by early afternoon, and rarely interact with anyone except mental health workers and other patients. Residents line up for medication, which they are made to ingest in public, and sometimes their mouths are checked as a precaution to prevent "cheeking" their pills. Many residents are heavily medicated, which interferes with socializing, working, and staying awake during the day. Coffee and soda are the most cherished beverages in these kinds of places, chasing the blues and offsetting the sedative effects of the medications. A weekly van ride to the mall, a movie, or a Chinese buffet may be the main difference between life in the hospital and life in a congregate care facility.

And these are some of the better facilities. In a Pulitzer Prize-winning series published in the *New York Times* in 2002, Clifford Levy documented hundreds of suspicious deaths between 1995 and 2001 in some of New York City's worst for-profit adult homes, including "some residents [who] died roasting in their rooms during heat waves. . . . Still more, lacking the most basic care, succumbed to routinely treatable ailments, from burst appendixes to seizures."

More than ten thousand people with psychiatric disabilities still lived in New York State's privately owned adult homes in 2007. While most of these places offer better conditions than the worst facilities described in Levy's articles, their residents are still largely cut off from the broader community. Most receive Social Security, of which the homes take the lion's share, leaving residents with about $50 per month. John, aged twenty-nine, spent most of his teens and twenties in and out of state hospitals and psychiatric wards. He describes a congregate living facility he was sent to in 2000:

> *My case manager took me to this home in Hempstead. It was a crack neighborhood, just really a run-down neighborhood. There was no air conditioning. There were roaches. There was no food. This was supposed to be my new home. They had this standing rule where you had to wake up at 6 o'clock in the morning, be out of your room, and they'd lock the door. I had nothing to do. It was the middle of summer. It was hot. I was exhausted from boredom. I was just very unhappy.*

Fortunately, there have been some positive developments in the housing area in recent years. In New York State, more subsidized independent housing has become available, in which people hold the leases to their own apartments and can use support services if they want them. A small number of low-interest mortgages with no down payment are offered to people with disabilities, enabling a few former psychiatric patients to buy their own homes. In some parts of the state, there is crisis respite housing, some even run by ex-patients, providing people in crisis a safe haven without being committed to a hospital and jeopardizing their housing. More alternatives like this are still needed; in many states, such options are entirely lacking.

TREATMENT

Medication is the foundation of modern psychiatry. For example, anyone diagnosed with psychosis or schizophrenia is immediately put on a neuroleptic drug with the goal of lifelong maintenance treatment. A recent study funded by the National Institute for Mental Health (NIMH) showed what many psychiatric patients have been reporting for years: the medications are not particularly effective and can cause serious, debilitating, even life-threatening side effects. Second generation neuroleptics, also called "atypicals," were considered more effective and less likely to cause side effects than the older drugs, which are significantly less expensive. The NIMH study showed that these highly praised medications were no more effective than the cheaper drugs they replaced, while causing a slew of new side effects, including diabetes and heart disease. A 2006 British study had similar results, and the researchers, who had expected the opposite outcome, were completely bewildered. "Why were we so convinced?" one of the researchers was quoted by the *Washington Post*. "I think pharmaceutical companies did a great job in selling their products." With this latest evidence, there is a need for serious discussions about the use and misuse of psychiatric drugs and the importance of effective alternative treatments. But because the system has become so heavily dominated by medication, such discussions seem unlikely.

Because of the persistent primacy of medication in psychiatry, today's patients not unlike the suitcase owners, are likely to find that their life circumstances are not considered particularly relevant by their psychiatrists. Sonia, first hospitalized as a homeless eighteen year old, was never asked at any hospital about her childhood:

> *I was an abandoned child, I was abandoned as a newborn at a church in Queens. The priest found me and I was taken to Elmhurst Hospital. And then after that I was in foster care. At an early age I used to isolate myself. Didn't talk to anybody. I used to do a lot of crying. I was mistreated, I was physically and mentally abused, raped. And when I was 16, I ran away and lived on the street.*

Recently, there has been a renewed emphasis on obtaining more indepth histories, especially concerning physical and sexual abuse, which the vast majority of people with the most serious diagnoses have experienced. There is an increasing awareness that even flagrant psychotic symptoms such as auditory hallucinations can be traced back to traumatic experiences. Such realizations point to the possibility that narrative accounts will become increasingly more important in treatment of people at risk for psychiatric hospitalization and drugging.

Access to services other than medication depends largely on where a person lives. In states with low per-capita spending, services may be limited to day programs that are primarily custodial in nature. In wealthier states like New York, people may have the chance for group or individual counseling, or help with getting their high school equivalency diploma or going to college. Many people now have opportunities for rehabilitation, rather than being exploited as institutional labor like some of the suitcase owners were. But real paying jobs are difficult to find in an economy that still discriminates; people with psychiatric disabilities have a staggering national unemployment rate of 90 percent, despite research showing that the vast majority are ready and eager to work.

Many of the problems faced by people with mental health histories are the same as those of other people in poverty: lack of access to decent housing, health care, dental care, and transportation; inadequate nutrition; lack of educational opportunities; under-employment and unemployment; and hopelessness and despair. People with psychiatric disabilities face additional challenges unique to their status as mental patients. A report by the National Council on Disability (NCD) calls the treatment of people with psychiatric disabilities "a national emergency and a national disgrace." The report says that "NCD heard testimony graphically describing how people have been beaten, shocked, isolated, incarcerated, restricted, raped, and physically and psychologically abused in institutions and in their communities. The testimony pointed to the inescapable fact that people with psychiatric disabilities are systematically and routinely deprived of their rights, and treated as less than full citizens or full human beings."

Nancy, a woman in her fifties who spent years in Willard and other hospitals, made this plea for decent treatment:

An area that really needs to be improved is the lack of sensitivity of the staff. No matter how out of it you may be, you're still a human being. You still have feelings and emotions and needs. And to treat you as if you don't matter, that's very detrimental to being healed emotionally. And even though you might be discharged, a series of those kinds of experiences, of being treated like an inanimate object, scars you to the point that you can't hold your head up when you walk down the street.

A MOVEMENT FOR HUMAN RIGHTS
IN THE MENTAL HEALTH SYSTEM

Madeline Cartier's unbending resistance is part of a long history; as long as there have been asylums and mental hospitals, there have been patients who are outraged about their confinement and the so-called treatment that they are offered. One nineteenth-century example is that of Elizabeth Ware Packard. Committed to an Illinois asylum in 1860 by her husband because of her "unorthodox" religious views, she carried her resistance from the back wards into court and was found "not insane" by a jury. She wrote several illustrated books describing abusive practices in the asylum, which resulted in official investigations and changes in the Illinois commitment law.

While the ex-patients' movement has roots in nineteenth-century social reform efforts and individual patients' struggles for justice, the modern movement began in earnest in the 1970s. Pioneering groups took their inspiration from other movements of disenfranchised people, such as the civil rights movement, the women's movement, and the disability movement. Like these groups, ex-patients and their allies are concerned with human and civil rights, with prejudice and discrimination, and they work toward a future in which the larger society will recognize the full humanity of people with psychiatric histories. As the movement developed, its members worked (and continue to work) for social, political, and legal equality; for the right to self-definition and self-determination; and for access to alternatives to the medical model of treatment. Over the past thirty-five years, the movement has evolved from a largely discounted fringe group to one that is poised to become a significant political force for change.

One result of this movement has been the development of peer support organizations, which allow people with psychiatric histories to give and receive help in a non-hierarchical atmosphere that promotes growth and well-being. Peer support in the medical arena is based on a shared experience of coping with illnesses such as cancer or heart attack. But in the mental health field, peer support grew out of the shared experience of negative events in treatment, such as coercion, disabling medication side effects, rights violations, and the dismissal of people's past histories of trauma. Mainstream mental health services, by promoting a pathology-based understanding of the self, often result in overwhelmingly negative self-appraisals. People may come to see themselves as passive and dependent mental patients and live their lives accordingly, nearly forgetting who they were prior to entering the psychiatric system. Peer support offers an alternative worldview of hope and self-determination for people whose personal struggles and emotional distress have been labeled as pathologies. It provides opportunities for people to reflect upon their life stories and upon the habits and values inculcated by their experiences with psychiatry. This process, which usually occurs outside the mental health system, can lead to a reconstruction of personal narratives in terms of healing and the possibility of a positive, self-determined future.

SOURCES CONSULTED

BOOKS AND ARTICLES

Abrams, Lynn. *The Orphan Country: Children of Scotland's Broken Homes, 1845 to the Present Day.* Edinburgh: John Donald, 1998.

Anda, R. F., Felitti, V. J. & Bremner, J. D., et. al. (2006) "The Enduring Effects of Abuse and Related Adverse Experiences in Childhood: A Convergence of Evidence from Neurobiology and Epidemiology." *European Archives of Psychiatry and Clinical Neuroscience, 256:3* 174–186.

Annual Reports of the Board of Managers of the Willard State Hospital to the State Commission in Lunacy, 1899–1945.

Annual Reports to the State Board of Charities by the Craig Colony for Epileptics at Sonyea in Livingston County, New York, 1897–1921.

Caplan, Paula J. *They Say You're Crazy: How the World's Most Powerful Psychiatrists Decide Who's Normal.* Boston: Addison-Wesley, 1995.

Chester, Phyllis. *Women and Madness.* New York: Doubleday, 1972.

Crane, George. (1973) "Clinical Psychopharmacology in Its 20th Year." *Science,* 181:121.

Danvers State Memorial Committee. "A History of Our Work." http://dsmc.info/work.shtml (accessed November 20, 2006).

Desai, M. M. & Rosenheck, R.A. (2003). "Trends in discharge disposition, mortality, and service use among long-stay psychiatric patients in the 1990s." *Psychiatric Services,* 54(4):542–8.

Deutsch, Albert. *The Mentally Ill in America: A History of Their Care and Treatment from Colonial Times.* 2d ed. New York: Columbia University Press, 1949.

―――. *The Shame of the States*. New York: Harcourt Brace, 1948.

Doran, Robert. *History of the Willard Asylum for the Insane and the Willard State Hospital*. Unpublished manuscript, 1978.

Dwyer, Ellen. *Homes for the Mad: Life Inside Two Nineteenth-Century Asylums*. New Brunswick, NJ: Rutgers University Press, 1987.

Fingal Community History Committee. *Fingal Community History*, 1980, Fingal, North Dakota.

Foley, Daniel, Manderscheid, Ronald & Atay, Joanne, et. al. "Highlights of Organized Mental Health Services in 2002 and Major National Trends." In *Mental Health United States 2004*. Manderscheid, Ronald and Berry, Joyce, eds. Washington, D.C.: U.S. Department of Health and Human Services, Substance Abuse and Mental Health Administration, Center for Mental Health Services.

Frank, Arthur. *The Wounded Storyteller: Body, Illness and Ethics*. Chicago: University of Chicago Press, 1995.

From Privileges to Rights: People Labeled with Psychiatric Disabilities Speak for Themselves. Washington, D.C.: National Council on Disability, 2002.

Gamwell, Lynn & Tomes, Nancy. *Madness in America: Cultural and Medical Perceptions of Mental Illness before 1914*. Ithaca, NY: Cornell University Press, 1995.

Goffman, Erving. *Asylums: Essays on the Social Situation of Mental Patients and Other Inmates*. New York, NY: Anchor Books/ Doubleday, 1961.

Gollaher, David L. *A Voice for the Mad: The Life of Dorothea Dix*. New York, NY: Free Press, 1994.

Grob, Gerald. *From Asylum to Community: Mental Health Policy in Modern America*. Princeton, NJ: Princeton University Press, 1991.

―――. *The Mad Among Us: A History of America's Care of the Mentally Ill*. New York: Free Press, 1994.

―――. (1985). "The Transformation of the Mental Hospital in the United States." *American Behavioral Scientist*. 28: 639-654.

Harding, C. & Zahniser, J. (1994). "Empirical Correction of Seven Myths About Schizophrenia with Implications for Treatment." *Acta Psychiatr Scand*, suppl. 384:140–146.

Harris, Maxine and Fallot, R.D. (2001) "Envisioning a Trauma-Informed

Service System: A Vital Paradigm Shift." *New Directions in Mental Health Services*; 89:3–22.

Hartmann, Sister Irene, O.P. *A Story of Mother Antonina Fischer, O.S.D., Foundress of the Dominican Sisters*. Self-published, Great Bend: KS, 1977.

Hegart, James, Baldessarini, Ross & Tohen, Mauricio, et al. (October 1994). "One Hundred Years of Schizophrenia: A Meta-analysis of the Outcome Literature." *American Journal of Psychiatry*, 151:10, 1409–1416.

Hoffman, J. L. (1943). "Psychotic Visitors to Government Offices in the National Capital." *American Journal of Psychiatry*, 99:571–5.

Honig, A., Romme, M. & Ensink, B., et al. (1998). "Auditory Hallucinations: A Comparison Between Patients and Nonpatients." *Journal of Nervous and Mental Disorders*, 186:10, 646–651.

Hornstein, Gail (January 25, 2002). "Narratives of Madness, as Told from Within." *The Chronicle of Higher Education*, B7.

Human Rights Watch. "U.S.: Number of Mentally Ill in Prisons Quadrupled." http://hrw.org/english/docs/2006/09/06/usdom14137_txt.htm (accessed December 23, 2006).

Jablensky, A., Sartorius, N. & Ernberg, G. et al. (1992). "Schizophrenia: Manifestations, Incidence and Course in Different Cultures, a World Health Organization Ten-Country Study." *Psychological Medicine*, (Monograph suppl.) 20:1–95.

James, Doris & Glaze, Lauren (September 2006). "Special Report: Mental Health Problems of Prison and Jail Inmates." Washington: D.C.: U.S. Department of Justice, Office of Justice Programs, Bureau of Justice Statistics. (NCJ 213600).

Kalinowsky, Lothar B. & Hoch, Paul H. *Shock Treatments and Other Somatic Procedures in Psychiatry*. New York, NY: Grune & Stratton, 1946.

Leff, J., Sartorius, N., Korten, A. & Ernberg, G. (1992). "The International Pilot Study of Schizophrenia: Five-Year Follow-Up Findings." *Psychological Medicine* 22:131–45.

Lerman, Hannah. *Pigeonholing Women's Misery: A History and Critical Analysis of the Psychodiagnosis of Women in the Twentieth Century*. New York, NY: Basic Books, 1996.

Levin, Aaron (September 2, 2005). "Rational Buildings Designed to 'Calm the Disorderly Mind.'" *Psychiatric News*. 40:7, 24.

Lieberman, Jeffrey, Stroup, Scott & McEvoy, Joseph, et al. (2005). "Effectiveness of Antipsychotic Drugs in Patients with Chronic Schizophrenia." *New England Journal of Medicine.* 353:1209–23.

Linkins, K., Lucca, A., Housman, M. & Smith, S. (2006). *Preadmission Screening and Resident Review (PASRR) and Mental Health Services for Persons in Nursing Facilities.* DHHS Pub. No. (SMA) 05-4039. Rockville, MD: Center for Mental Health Services, Substance Abuse and Mental Health Services Administration.

Lovell, A.M. (June 1997). "The City Is My Mother: Narratives of Schizophrenia and Homelessness." *American Anthropologist,* 99, 2:355–368.

Mehr, Joseph. *An Illustrated History of Illinois Public Mental Health Services, 1847–2000.* Victoria, B.C., Canada: Trafford Publishing, 2002.

Morrissey, Joseph & Goldman, Howard (1986). "Care and Treatment of the Mentally Ill in the United States: Historical Developments and Reforms." *Annals of the American Academy of Political and Social Science.* The Law and Mental Health: Research and Policy, 484: 12–27.

———. (1984). "Cycles of Reform in the Care of the Chronically Mentally Ill." *Hospital and Community Psychiatry* 35:785–793.

Pollock, Horatio M., ed. *Family Care of Mental Patients: A Review of Systems of Family Care in America and Europe.* Utica, NY: State Hospitals Press, 1936.

Porter, Roy. *A Social History of Madness.* London, UK: Weidenfeld and Nicolson, 1987.

President's New Freedom Commission on Mental Health. *Achieving the Promise: Transforming Mental Health Care in America. Final Report.* DHHS Pub. No. SMA-03-3832. Rockville, MD: Department of Health and Human Services, 2003.

Ridgway, Priscilla (2001). "Restorying Psychiatric Disability: Learning from First Person Recovery Narratives." *Psychiatric Rehabilitation Journal,* 24(4):335–343.

Romme, Marius.(Summer 2000). "Redefining Hearing Voices." [From a speech given to the Hearing Voices Network] http://www.psychminded.co.uk /critical/marius.htm (accessed April 25, 2007).

Romme. M. A. & Escher, S., editors. *Accepting Voices.* London: Mind, 1993.

Rosenheck, R. (2000). "The Delivery of Mental Health Services in the 21st Century: Bringing the Community Back In." *Community Mental Health Journal,* 36(1):107-24.

Scull, Andrew (1990). "Deinstitutionalization: Cycles of Despair." *Journal of Mind and Behavior* 11(3):301–311.

Showalter, Elaine (1980). "Victorian Women and Insanity." *Victorian Studies,* 23(2):157–81.

Tomes, Nancy. *The Art of Asylum-Keeping: Thomas Story Kirkbride and the Origins of American Psychiatry.* Philadelphia, PA: University of Pennsylvania Press, 1994.

Webster's New World Medical Dictionary. 2nd ed. Chicago: Wiley Publishing, Inc., 2003.

Whitaker, Robert (Spring 2005). "Anatomy of an Epidemic: Psychiatric Drugs and the Astonishing Rise of Mental Illness in America." *Ethical Human Psychology and Psychiatry* 7(1):23–35.

———. *Mad in America: Bad Science, Bad Medicine, and the Enduring Mistreatment of the Mentally Ill.* Cambridge, MA: Perseus Publishing, 2002.

———. (2004). "The Case Against Antipsychotic Drugs: A 50-Year Record of Doing More Harm than Good." *Medical Hypotheses* 62:5–13.

CASE FILES

Charles F., case file #27976, Willard Psychiatric Center Patient Records, series 14231-95. New York State Archives, Albany, NY.

Dmytre Z., case file #32643, Willard Psychiatric Center Patient Records, series 14231-95. New York State Archives, Albany, NY.

Ethel S., case file #20756, Willard Psychiatric Center Patient Records, series 14231-95. New York State Archives, Albany, NY.

Frank C., case file #27967, Willard Psychiatric Center Patient Records, series 14231-95. New York State Archives, Albany, NY.

Frieda B., case file #22244, Willard Psychiatric Center Patient Records, series 14231-95. New York State Archives, Albany, NY

Herman G., case file #20894, Willard Psychiatric Center Patient Records, series 14231-95.New York State Archives, Albany, NY.

Josephine S., case file #08575, Willard Psychiatric Center Patient Records, series 14231-95. New York State Archives, Albany, NY

Irma M., case file #22985, Willard Psychiatric Center Patient Records, series 14231-95. New York State Archives, Albany, NY.

Lawrence M., case file #14956, Willard Psychiatric Center Patient Records, series 14231-95. New York State Archives, Albany, NY.

Madeline C., case file # 22040. Willard Psychiatric Center Patient Records, series 14231-95.New York State Archives, Albany, NY.

Margaret D., case file #25682, Willard Psychiatric Center Patient Records, series 14231-95. New York State Archives, Albany, NY.

Marie L., case file # 15468, Willard Psychiatric Center Patient Records, series 14231-95. New York State Archives, Albany, NY.

Rodrigo L., case file #15902, Willard Psychiatric Center Patient Records, series 14231-95. New York State Archives, Albany, NY.

INTERVIEWS

Donna Gustafson Cerza, R.N., interviewed by Darby Penney, September 15, 2004.

Jessica, interviewed by Jeanne Dumont for the Consumer/Survivor/Ex-patient Oral History Project, July 31, 2001, tape and transcript deposited at the New York State Archives.

John F., interviewed by Terry Strecker for the Consumer/Survivor /Ex-patient Oral History Project, January 18, 2001, tape and transcript deposited at the New York State Archives.

Laverne Dratt, R.N., interviewed by Steven Periard for the Consumer/ Survivor/Ex-patient Oral History Project, March 13, 2003, tape and transcript deposited at the New York State Archives.

Marie Schmidt, R.N., interviewed by Darby Penney for the Consumer /Survivor/Ex-patient Oral History Project, March 13, 2003, tape and transcript deposited at the New York State Archives.

Nancy (pseudonym), interviewed by Jeanne Dumont for the Consumer /Survivor/Ex-patient Oral History Project, August 25, 2000, tape and transcript deposited at the New York State Archives.

Nancy Jaycot Caniff, interviewed by Darby Penney and Steven Periard for the Consumer/Survivor/Ex-patient Oral History Project, March 13, 2003, tape and transcript deposited at the New York State Archives.

Sonia C., interviewed by Terry Strecker for the Consumer/Survivor/Ex-patient Oral History Project, July 26, 2001, tape and transcript deposited at the New York State Archives.

Victor F., interviewed by Steven Periard for the Consumer/Survivor/Ex-patient Oral History Project, November 1, 2002, tape and transcript deposited at the New York State Archives.

Web Rankin, R.N., interviewed by Darby Penney for the Consumer/Survivor /Ex-patient Oral History Project, March 13, 2003, tape and transcript deposited at the New York State Archives.

ACKNOWLEDGMENTS

This book is the result of almost ten years of research, writing, and photographic documentation that involved the efforts of many people. The authors thank everyone who contributed to the work of the Willard Suitcase Project. We especially want to recognize the contributions of:

Beverly Courtwright and Lisa Hoffman, who discovered the suitcases in the attic;

Craig Williams, Senior Historian at the New York State Museum, whose years of tireless work on the suitcase project made everything else possible;

Lisa Rinzler, whose stunning photographs documented the suitcases, their contents, and their surroundings;

Gene McKay, exhibit designer; Connie Houde, textile restorer; and Peggy Ross, translator, of the New York State Museum;

Kathleen Roe, Chief of Archival Services at the New York State Archives, whose enthusiastic support and encouragement were invaluable;

Jim Folts, Head of Researcher Services and his staff of archivists at the New York State Archives;

Aida Santos Mattingly of the Filipino-American Historical Society;

James Stone, former Commissioner of the New York State Office of Mental Health for his personal interest and support;

Joanne Atay, Daniel Foley, and Ingrid Goldstrum of the Statistics Branch of the Federal Center for Mental Health Services and Ted Lutterman of the NASMHPD Research Institute, for providing statistical data;

George Badillo for translating Spanish documents;

Jeanne Dumont, Steven Periard, and the late Terry Strecker for collecting many of the oral histories we quoted;

Robert Whitaker, whose work inspired us, and who wrote a wonderful foreword;

Steven Litt, for designing the hauntingly beautiful website, www.SuitcaseExhibit.org;

Ted Anderson and Donna Ostraszewski of The Exhibition Alliance;

The Nathan Cummings Foundation and The vanAmeringen Foundation for their generous support; and

Erika Goldman, our editor at Bellevue Literary Press, for her patience, counsel, and belief in the book.

In addition, Darby Penney wants to thank:

Ken Denberg, for believing in me and in the project;

Katherine Ambrosio, Ron Bassman, Dorothy Dundas, and Laura Prescott for their encouragement, comments, and insights; and

Patricia Deegan, whose pioneering work on the history of psychiatry from the patients' perspective was an inspiration for the project.

And Peter Stastny wishes to thank:

Iona Aibel and Mia Chiara Aibel Stastny for their unswerving support;

Anne Lovell and Kim Hopper for their insights and encouragement; and

JD Foster and Laura Israel for helping to put it all together.

INDEX

Page references in *italics* refer to illustrations.